# Geography in Action

**Series Editor**

Andy Owen — Head of Geography, The Community College, Bishop's Castle, Shropshire

**Authors**

Peter Bond — George Abbot School, Guildford

Peter Capener — Education Co-ordinator, Centre for Sustainable Energy, Bristol

Peter Jackson — Harrow School, London

Andy Owen — The Community College, Bishop's Castle

Graham Yates — Ryton Comprehensive School, Gateshead

Heinemann

Heinemann Educational Publishers
a division of Heinemann Publishers (Oxford) Ltd
Halley Court, Jordan Hill, Oxford OX2 8EJ

MADRID ATHENS PARIS FLORENCE PRAGUE WARSAW
PORTSMOUTH NH CHICAGO SAO PAULO
SINGAPORE TOKYO MELBOURNE AUCKLAND
IBADAN GABORONE JOHANNESBURG

© Peter Bond, Peter Capener, Peter Jackson, Andy Owen, Graham Yates, 1995

First published 1995

99 98
10 9 8 7 6 5 4

ISBN 0 435 35134 6

Designed and produced by Gecko Ltd, Bicester, Oxon

Cover photos by Science Photo Library/Novosti Press Agency (left); South American Pictures/Tony Morrison (right)
Geography is the study of people and the environment. Geographers study different places.
The smaller photograph shows the eruption of lava from a Japanese volcano. Brazil is a country where the difference
between rich and poor people is very great. The larger photograph shows the variety of housing available to people
in the second largest city, Rio de Janeiro.

Printed in Spain by Mateu Cromo Artes Graficas SA

## Acknowledgements

The authors and publishers would like to thank the following for permission to use photographs/copyright material (the numbers
refer to the pages on which material appears):

ActionAid, *Common Cause*: extracts 7, 77; *BBC Wildlife*: extract, 71; *Belize Review*: extract, 76; CPA Family Polling Studies Centre: table, 16; bar chart (source
Eurostat) 15; *The Daily Telegraph*: extract reproduced by permission of Ewan McNaughton Associates, 45; *The Economist*/Petrobras: advertisement, 87;
Edward Arnold Publishers Ltd: M.Witherick and M.Carr, *The Changing Face of Japan*, map, 46, diagram, 49; Escritt, E. A: map, 81; *Financial Times*: graphs
24.2.94, 32 (source Barings), 2.11.92/1.3.95, 46, 1.3.95, 70, table 17.11.94, 47, extract 13.3.92, 89; Geographical Association: *Teaching Geography*, Momsen,
graph, 83; table, 84; *The Guardian*: diagram, 25, extracts 32, 37, 92; Guardian Education: extract, 84, data for table 85; HarperCollins: Andrew Reed, *Issues in
Development*: Brazil, Unwin Hyman, page 88; HMSO, © Crown copyright is reproduced with the permission of the Controller of HMSO, map, 24, from *Global
Climate Change* 2nd Edition table, 52, map, 53; *Hong Kong Year Book*: graph, 36; *The Independent on Sunday*: extract, 13, 73, graph, 49; *The Independent*: extracts
by T McCarthy-Manila, 20, diagram, 44, map, 54, extract, 54; Longman: Knapp, Ross & McCare, *Challenge of the Human Environment*, pie chart, 9; Michelin:
map, 63; National Power plc: data for table, 56; *New Internationalist*: Geographical Studies of Development 12/79, diagram, 17; *New Scientist*: map, 25; Ordnance
Survey: Reproduced from the Ordnance Survey mapping with the permission of The Controller of HMSO © Crown Copyright, map, 78; Philip Allan
Publishers: *Geography Review*, map, 64, diagram, 58, graph, 74; School of Geography and Earth Resources: *Geography*, map, 16; Shobunsha Co. Ltd, Tokyo:
map, 41; Shropshire Star Newspapers Ltd: extract, 45; Stanley Thorne, Steve Scoble, *Area Resource Pack*: Brazil: table, 86, map, 89; © Times Newspapers
Limited 30.06.91: map 'Danger area: The Fens are now under serious threat from flooding' by Gunter Greatwood *Sunday Times Magazine*, 53; Thompson Tour
Operations Ltd: extract, graph, 73; UNEP: *World Atlas of Desertification*, 67; World Bank Atlas: map, 14; World Resource Foundation: extract, 42.

### Photographs

ActionAid: 6/Liba Taylor, 7T/Morris Keyonzo, 7B/Jenny Matthews, 17/K. Ponnappa Subbaiah, 77B/Adam Hinton; Associated Press/Topham Picture Library:
10 & 20T, 25/G. Ramesh, 57; Peter Capener: 60 all; Christian Aid Photo Library: 91/E. Berrios; Coral Cay Conservation Ltd: 79 both; Gertrud and Helmut
Denzau: 71; Environmental Picture Library: 42/Steve Morgan, 54T/Bob Edward, 54B/Roger Grace, 55/Paul Glendell; Friends of the Earth: 61R; Peter Furley:
74, 75, 78; Robert Harding Picture Library: 9 & 12/J. H. C. Wilson, 14L/Sassoon, 14R/James Strachan, 26/Gavin Hellier, 32/David Lomax, 40, 48/Elly
Beintema, 64, 83L/C Bowman; The Hutchison Library: 30/R. Ian Lloyd, 31, 46/Michael MacIntyre; Peter Jackson: 80; David Job: 58; Frank Lane Picture
Agency: 23/S. Jonasson, 66/David Hosking, 76B/Terry Whittaker; Magnum Photos: 36T/Patrick Zachmann, 36B & 69/Ian Berry, 84/Bruno Barbey; Janet
Momsen: 35; David Munro: 76T, 77T; Mark Newham/Eye Ubiquitous: 62; NHPA: 90/Jany Sauvanet/E. Janes, 92T/Gerard Lacz; Andy Owen: 59; Panos
Pictures: 33/Chris Stowers, 70/Roderick Johnson, 83R/Sean Sprague; Popperfoto: 18, 44R/Reuter; Carlos Reyes/Andes Press Agency: 85; Science Photo
Library/NASA: 20B, 34, 61L; Spectrum Colour Library: 38/Raga; Frank Spooner Pictures: 92B/J. L. Bulcao; Still Pictures: 67/Mark Edwards, 93/John Maier;
Thomson Worldwide, 1993: 73 both; Topham Picture Library: 27; Cynthia Widden: 44L.

The publishers have made every effort to trace the copyright holders, but if they have inadvertently overlooked any, they will be pleased to make the
necessary arrangements at the first opportunity.

# **H**ow to use this book

## Location globe

This is a map of the world. It shows you where the country you are studying is.

## Unit aims

At the start of each unit the key ideas are clearly set out. These are the unit aims.

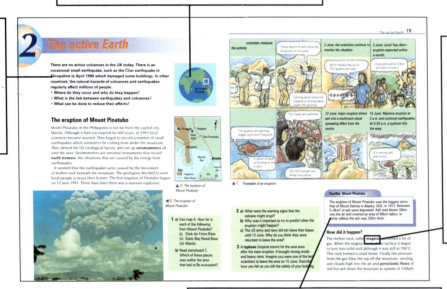

## Keywords

Important geographical words are printed in **bold** type. They are listed and explained at the back of the book in the **Glossary** on pages 94–95.

## Factfile

This includes extra information about the place or topic being covered.

## Captions

A caption appears next to each picture, map, diagram, graph, and newspaper article. The ▶ points to the source the caption describes. The letter helps you to find the right source when answering the questions.

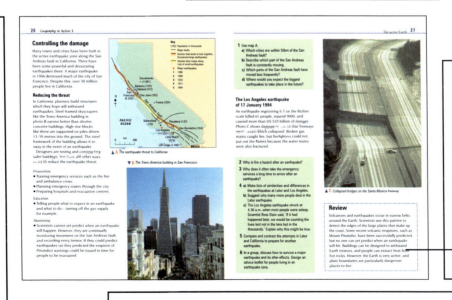

## Review

At the end of each unit there is a Review. This provides a summary of the key ideas you have studied in the unit. It is useful to read this before you move on to the next unit.

## Index

The Index on page 96 lists the topics, places, and ideas covered in the book. It gives you the page numbers where they are explained or described.

# Contents

# 7 Population

In this unit we will be finding answers to the following questions:
- why do people in some countries have many children?
- what special contribution do children make?
- why is birth control an important issue?
- what happens as people live longer and there are many older people in the population?

## Youthful populations

Women in developing countries have more children than women in the developed world. The large proportion of children in these countries gives them what is called a **youthful population**. Graph A shows the proportion of children in India and the UK.

## Children work for a living

At least 44 million children in India go to work, and there are many more who are missed out of surveys. Most work in factories and on farms, but others break stones or do **informal** work such as rag-picking. More than 100 000 children work in Bangalore and Bombay (Mumbai) as rag-pickers. They search through waste on refuse dumps to find materials that can be sold, recycled or reused. It is a dirty and dangerous job, but it saves valuable resources, and helps keep the city streets clean. Rag-pickers need to collect the equivalent of a stack of paper one metre high to earn 20 rupees (40 pence) a day in order to survive.

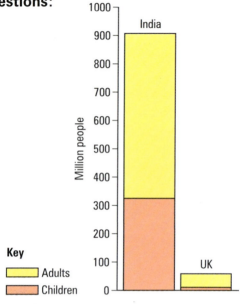

▲ **A** The population of India and the UK compared

---

**1** Use graph A.
   **a)** How many children live in India?
   **b)** How does this compare to the total population of the UK?
   **c)** How does the proportion of children in India compare to the proportion of children in the UK?

---

My name is Sampangi. I am 17 and I live in a hostel for homeless children in Bangalore, India. I've no parents. Before I came here, I was on the road, rag-picking. I did it every day to make enough money to eat and see a movie. I slept anywhere I could find a place. Sometimes the cops would chase me away or older boys would steal my things.

▶ **B** Sampangi, a rag-picker in Bangalore

## Children support their families

◀ **C** *Naiga and her sister live in Uganda*

The two girls in photo C are sisters. They live in Uganda. Their parents have died of AIDS. Naiga, on the right, is only 14. Since her parents died she has dropped out of school and is now caring for three younger brothers and sisters. About 1 in 7 adults in Naiga's village have AIDS. Estimates vary, but in July 1993, it was thought that there were at least 100 000 AIDS orphans, and about 1.5 million Ugandans who have the HIV virus, which causes AIDS. Mothers with the virus often pass it on to their children.

**2 a)** Describe the difficulties faced by child workers like Sampangi.

**b)** Who relies on Sampangi and Naiga?

**c)** Naiga is often bullied by local boys who see that she is alone. This makes her very depressed. Discuss this issue in a small group. What advice can you give to people who are bullied?

**3** Create captions for photos C and D that will:

**a)** raise awareness of the problems faced by the world's children

**b)** draw attention to the value and resourcefulness of these children.

**4** *How would you survive if you were a rag-picker? Design a toy using common scrap materials.*

## Children at play

You can't buy a truck like this in the shops at any price. It cost Christopher Luka, from Malawi, a great deal of time, thought and effort to create a model he was proud of. Wood is scarce in many African countries so children use old tin cans, bottle tops and pieces of wire to make their toys.

▲ **D** *From* **Common Cause**, *January 1994*

# Children of the world

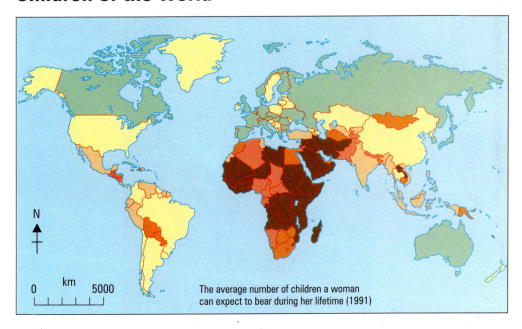

The average number of children a woman can expect to bear during her lifetime (1991)

◀ **A** *How average family size varies from country to country*

**Key**

| | |
|---|---|
| ■ | 6 children or more |
| ■ | 5 children or more |
| ■ | 4 children or more |
| ■ | 3 children or more |
| ■ | 2 children or more |
| ■ | 1 child |

▼ **B** *The average wealth (Gross National Product, GNP) of selected countries, in US $ per person*

Map A shows that women in developing countries have more children. Why is this?

**1** Use map A.
  **a)** What is the average family size in Europe?
  **b)** Which continent has most countries with a large average family size?

**2 a)** Use graph B to find the average wealth (GNP) in Japan, Brazil, and Bangladesh.

  **b)** Compare the wealth shown in graph B to the average family size in the same three countries. Can you see any connection between the map and the graph? Describe the pattern that exists, using Japan, Brazil, and Bangladesh as examples.

**3** Why would it be difficult to read the GNP for these countries from an ordinary bar chart? (It might help to try drawing one.)

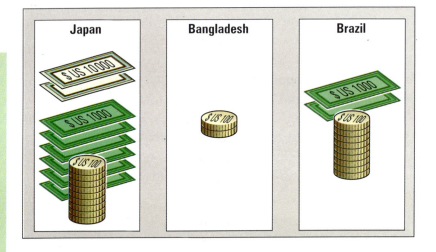

| Country | Infant mortality* | Family size |
|---|---|---|
| Afghanistan | 162 | 6+ |
| Bangladesh | 108 | |
| Nigeria | 96 | |
| Uganda | 94 | |
| India | 88 | |
| Kenya | 64 | |
| Brazil | 57 | |
| Mexico | 36 | |
| Argentina | 29 | |
| Spain | 9 | |
| UK | 8 | |
| Japan | 5 | |

◀ **C** *Child deaths in every 1000 people*

\* infant mortality is the number of children who die before the age of one, for every 1000 that are born.

THIMMAKKA    We have two pairs of bullocks and two fields. We need the help of our children to work on the land. So how can I send them all to school? This work has to be done so that we can all eat.

PONNUTHI    I disagree. Children deserve to be educated so that they get a chance in life.

MEERA    Ponnuthi is right, but with four very young children, I need the help of my eldest daughter around the house, and to care for the toddlers when I am busy. I will send the boys to school.

THIMMAKKA    Absolutely. Why should my daughter be educated? After all she will soon get married and go to her husband's house.

PONNUTHI    That's where you're wrong. Whether they are boys or girls they should study. I have four girls and they are all in school. We have taken many loans and we are struggling, but so what?

INDIRA    You are all so lucky. Both my children died before they were five. Now my husband and I have no help. Who will look after us when we are too old to work?

The conversation of the four Indian women above shows us that children can be of help to their families in many ways. Poor people in some countries choose to have many children. The children go out to work and bring in more money for the family. They also help with household chores and work on the family farm. Poverty can lead to larger families, not the other way round. Diagram D reminds us that parents have different reasons for having children.

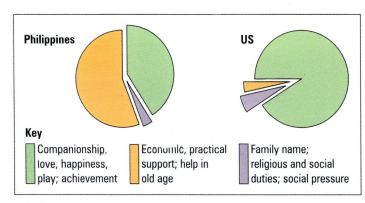

Key

- Companionship, love, happiness, play; achievement
- Economic, practical support; help in old age
- Family name; religious and social duties; social pressure

▲ **D** *How children are valued*

**4** List all the reasons why these women want to have large families. You should find at least three.

**5** Why do you think wealthy families, even in India, are likely to have fewer children?

**6** a) Make a copy of table C in your book. Complete the table by finding the average family size in each country by using map A. The first one has been done for you.

b) Try to explain the pattern shown in the table.

**7** Imagine you were part of the women's conversation. What would you say to them about children in the UK, especially about school, work, and families? Continue the conversation in your book, keeping what each woman says true to her character.

# Variations in family size

We have seen that India has a youthful population because most women have several children. India is said to have a high **birth rate**. However, even within India there are variations in the birth rate, as map A shows. One reason for this is that in some states people have children at a very young age.

**▲ A** *Regional variations in India's birth rate*

Key
Birth rate (per 1000)
More than 38
33.5–37.9
Average for India (33.5)
29–33.4
Less than 29
**N.D.** No data

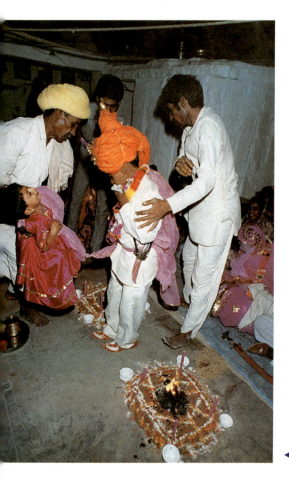

**◀ B** *A child marriage in Rajasthan*

Child marriage is an ancient custom in some rural parts of India. It is supposed to be illegal, but a recent survey found that 90 per cent of girls in the states of Rajasthan and Andhra Pradesh were already married by the age of 15. Many children die in rural India so it is quite possible for a young girl to be widowed before she is 16. Widows are not allowed to remarry. Many run away to the city, or have to beg to make a living.

**1** Use map A.
  **a)** List the Indian states that have the highest birth rates.
  **b)** Describe any pattern you can see in the birth rate. Using points of the compass, describe the parts of India with higher and lower birth rates.

## Asha: the story of a young widow

Asha works as a maid for a rich businessman in Delhi. She ran away from her home in the country when she was 15. Asha had been married to a local boy when she was 9, although she continued to live with her parents. At the age of 14 she was about to join her husband and his family when he died, and she became a widow.

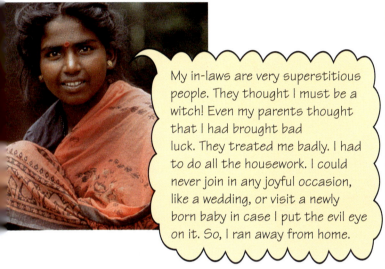

> My in-laws are very superstitious people. They thought I must be a witch! Even my parents thought that I had brought bad luck. They treated me badly. I had to do all the housework. I could never join in any joyful occasion, like a wedding, or visit a newly born baby in case I put the evil eye on it. So, I ran away from home.

▲ **C** *Asha explains how her husband's death affected her*

## Reducing the birth rate in Kerala

Not all Indian states have a high birth rate. In Kerala the birth rate has been falling for years. As the health official below explains, this is a result of improved health care and education.

> In Kerala as many women as men go to school and university. We have found that women's education and health care have cut family sizes. If you provide health care to bring down infant mortality, then people accept that a small family is normal and the birth rate will come down.

▲ **D** *Health official in Kerala, south-west India*

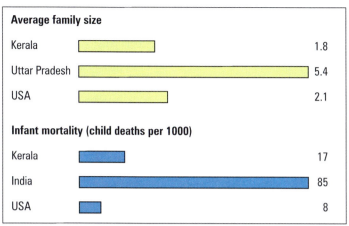

| Average family size | | |
|---|---|---|
| Kerala | | 1.8 |
| Uttar Pradesh | | 5.4 |
| USA | | 2.1 |

| Infant mortality (child deaths per 1000) | | |
|---|---|---|
| Kerala | | 17 |
| India | | 85 |
| USA | | 8 |

▲ **E** *How Kerala compares*

**2 a)** Explain why Asha ran away from home. You might mention both superstition and the way she was treated.

**b)** What do you think would have happened to Asha if she had stayed in the village?

**c)** Why might an early marriage lead to a woman having many children?

**3** What colour would you expect to be shown on map A for these two states, and why?

**a)** Rajasthan (where Asha lived)

**b)** Kerala.

**4** Look back through pages 6 to 11.

**a)** Produce a report listing the reasons why people in India have large families.

**b)** Explain what effect the high birth rate has on children. You could mention Sampangi or Asha as examples.

## Summary

We have learned so far that people in developing countries have children for many reasons.
- Poor parents expect children to help earn money for the family. Children help on the farm or in the family business. They also look after younger children, and sick or elderly parents.
- An early marriage means more chance of a big family.
- Where child deaths are common, parents are likely to have several children, in case one or more die.

# Reducing India's birth rate

The Indian government has been trying for some years to encourage people to have smaller families. They are worried that if the birth rate is not brought down, the country will not be able to feed or house all its people. **Family planning** is also a vital issue to ordinary people.

| THIMMAKKA | I don't want any more children. But my husband won't listen when I start talking about family planning. He wants another son to work on the farm. |
|---|---|
| PONNUTHI | Perhaps you should ask the health worker to talk to him about being sterilized. |
| THIMMAKKA | You're joking! He'd never do that. |
| MEERA | My husband says that sterilization would make him weak or something. |
| INDIRA | My uncle had no choice. He was forced to have the operation during the Emergency. All he got was a cheap transistor radio! |
| PONNUTHI | Well, there are other methods of birth control. When I went into town last month I saw shops there selling nothing but condoms. You know what else, I bought some! |

| MEERA | I wouldn't dare to even go near a shop like that. Anyway, I don't suppose I could even afford them. How much did they cost? |
|---|---|
| PONNUTHI | Only half a rupee [about 1p] for three. |
| THIMMAKKA | Well, that's no use to me. I've never even been to town. |
| INDIRA | Why is it always the women who have to think about family planning? I got sterilized, and look what happened to me. Both of my children died, and now I can't have any more. |

▲ **A** *Opinions vary about family planning*

In 1975 emergency laws were brought in. Men were forced (at gunpoint on some occasions) to be sterilized. Nowadays, the government does its best to persuade women to agree to sterilization. Schools are converted into makeshift hospitals for a day or two. The women arrive by the jeep load. The operation is over in 45 seconds, and then the women lie in rows in the schoolroom recovering from the painful experience. The government offers 200 rupees (£4) to any woman who has the operation. In 1993 about 4.1 million women were sterilized, mainly older women who already had several children.

On a main New Delhi boulevard, next to a huge advertisement for a brand of condoms, you find India's population clock. Its green digital numbers glow with the arrival of a new baby every 1.5 seconds. By the time the boulevard light has changed, another 35 babies have been born. A similar clock in Peking would count 33 births a minute, while in London you might miss the green light waiting for the birth of a Briton.

India's population control efforts have so far failed, and future attempts may be doomed. The best contraceptive, social workers have found, is not the condom or the IUD. It is female literacy. Yet now the Indian government, under pressure from the World Bank and the IMF to cut spending, has lopped off funds for medical care and education.

As one international health worker said: 'You could fill up a plane with condoms, fly over India and dump them out, but that wouldn't help if people down below don't have a clue what they're for.'

Couples living in high literacy states, such as Kerala, tend to have only two children, while in more populous states where fewer can read, families have more than five children. However, the population clock in New Delhi is not going to stand still while India dithers over educating its poor.

▲ **B** *Extract from* The Independent on Sunday, *15 November 1992*

|  | 1950 | 1960 | 1970 | 1980 | 1990 |
|---|---|---|---|---|---|
| **Birth rate (per 1000 people)** | 44 | 42 | 38 | 35 | 31 |
| **Death rate (per 1000 people)** | 25 | 19 | 16 | 13 | 10 |

▲ **C** *India's birth and **death rates** (1950–1990)*

**1 a)** Use the information in table C to draw a line graph. It should have two lines, one for births and one for deaths.
   **b)** Describe the path, or trend, of each line.
   **c)** Describe what happens to the gap between the two lines.

**2** Read carefully what the women in A said.
   **a)** Discuss in a small group the effect of each of the following on family planning:
   (i)   superstition and ignorance
   (ii)  wealth or poverty
   (iii) availability of contraceptives.
   **b)** Choose two of the above and write about how they affect the decisions people make about family planning.

**3** Look back at page 11. How has Kerala been successful in reducing the birth rate?

**4** Read extract B. Do you think India has a good birth control policy? How would you advise the Indian government to control the birth rate?

**5 a)** Use graph D to find the family size and percentage of females in secondary education in:

   (i) Japan   (ii) Brazil   (iii) India   (iv) Ghana.

   **b)** *What does this graph tell us about the importance of equal opportunities for women?*

▼ **D** *Fertility and education*

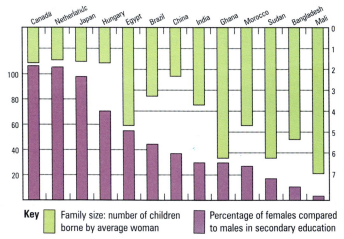

Key — Family size: number of children borne by average woman — Percentage of females compared to males in secondary education

# The world's ageing population

In most countries, people now live longer than in the past, mostly because of better health care.

The average age to which people live is known as **life expectancy**. As map A shows, life expectancy is highest in the developed countries.

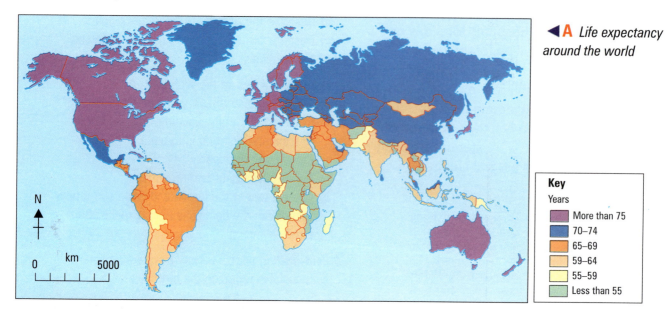

◀ **A** *Life expectancy around the world*

**Key**

Years

| | |
|---|---|
| | More than 75 |
| | 70–74 |
| | 65–69 |
| | 59–64 |
| | 55–59 |
| | Less than 55 |

▼ **B** *D'igir Turoga is 58*

I have herded camels and goats all my life. Younger people have settled in the town, they have forgotten the old ways. I can still make my living herding. I can still find water under ground even before the scientists from the Aid Project can find it with their equipment.

▼ **C** *Mama Ndoga is 70*

I still help at harvest. I carry a sack of pineapples back from the fields just like anyone else. I love to look after my grandchildren and great-grandchildren who all live in my home village.

▼ **D** *Some changes in life expectancy*

| Country | 1950–55 | | 1970–75 | | 1990–95 | |
|---|---|---|---|---|---|---|
| **List 1** | male | female | male | female | male | female |
| Afghanistan | 31 | 32 | 38 | 38 | 43 | 44 |
| Bangladesh | 38 | 35 | 46 | 44 | 53 | 53 |
| Brazil | 49 | 53 | 58 | 62 | 64 | 69 |
| Kenya | 39 | 43 | 49 | 53 | 59 | 63 |
| **List 2** | | | | | | |
| Japan | 62 | 66 | 71 | 76 | 76 | 82 |
| Spain | 62 | 66 | 70 | 76 | 74 | 80 |
| UK | 67 | 72 | 69 | 75 | 73 | 79 |
| USA | 66 | 72 | 68 | 75 | 73 | 80 |

**1** Use map A. Find average life expectancy in:
 a) UK b) India c) Kenya

**2** Use table D.
 a) Draw bar graphs to show how life expectancy has changed in one country from list 1, and one from list 2.
 b) Describe the trends shown on your graphs.

**3** D'igir Turoga reminds us that older people have much to offer the community.
 a) Use B and C to list the ways in which elderly people help us, under the headings:
 **Knowledge  Experience  Skills**
 b) Think about elderly people you know. What else can you add to your list?

# The changing European population

As people in Europe have become richer, they have had fewer children. They no longer need children to help earn money for the family. Life expectancy has also improved. So, as people live to be older, and they also have fewer children, the proportions of young and elderly people are changing.

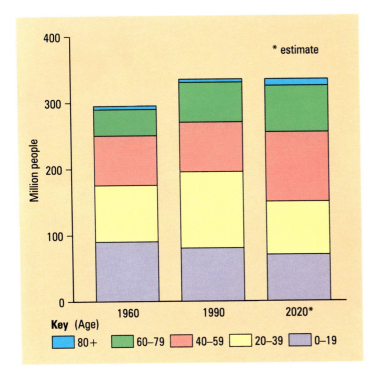

▲ **E** *How Europe's population is changing*

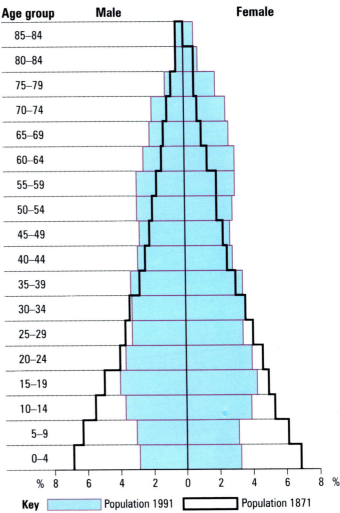

▲ **F** *How the UK's population has changed*

4 Study graph E.
  a) Describe what is happening to the number of children.
  b) How many people were over 60 in 1960?
  c) How many people will be over 60 in 2020?

5 Using diagram F, describe how the proportion of each of the following has changed:
  a) younger people
  b) adults of working age
  c) elderly people.

6 People under 15 and over 65 are sometimes called **dependants**.
  a) Discuss in what ways these age groups depend on others. Make a list in your book.
  b) Do you think D'igir Turoga and Mama Ndoga are dependent on younger people? Explain your answer carefully.
  c) From what you have learned about children in India, is it true that all children are dependent on adults?

7 *Were families bigger in the past than they are now? Do some research into your own family. How many children are there in your generation, and how many were there in your parents' generation, and their parents' generation?*

# Retirement in the UK

At the age of 60 or 65 most people retire and are entitled to a **state pension**. Some people also receive money from private or company pension schemes that they paid in to while they were working.

|  | Employment | State pensions | Occupational/private pensions | Savings | Other |
|---|---|---|---|---|---|
| Germany | 21 | 34 | 34 | 11 | - |
| Italy | 1 | 46 | 49 | 2 | 2 |
| Portugal | 14 | 58 | - | 7 | 21 |
| UK | 8 | 50 | 25 | 17 | - |
| Luxembourg | 6 | 92 | - | 1 | 1 |

▲ **A** *Sources of income of people over 60 in Europe (percentages)*

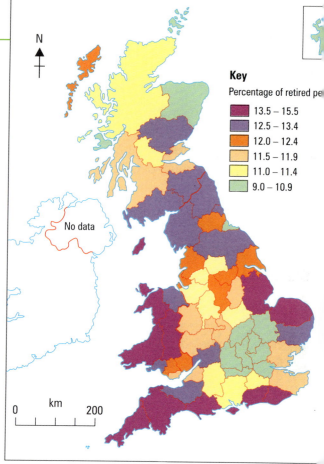

**Key**
Percentage of retired pe...
- 13.5 – 15.5
- 12.5 – 13.4
- 12.0 – 12.4
- 11.5 – 11.9
- 11.0 – 11.4
- 9.0 – 10.9

No data

km
0    200

▶ **B** *Distribution of retired people in UK*

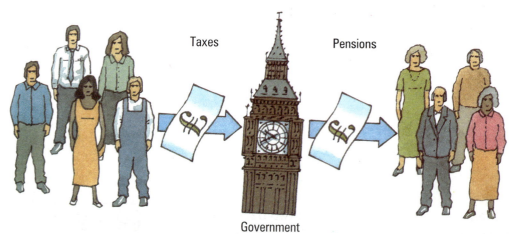

Taxes    Pensions

Government

◀ **C** *How the government pays pensions*

**1** Using map B, work out which parts of the UK have:
   **a)** less than 11 per cent retired population
   **b)** over 13.5 per cent retired population.

**2** The governments of European countries worry that they will not be able to continue to pay state pensions. Using diagram C above and graph E on page 15, explain why governments are worried about an ageing population. Try to predict what might happen in the future, by the year 2020.

**3 a)** Use table A to draw divided bars to show the sources of income of people over 60 in these countries.
   **b)** Which of these countries will have to make the biggest changes to support its elderly population?

**4** *In India a health worker said, 'It is up to the sons, not the Indian state, to look after parents when they grow old.' Explain what this means. How is it different in Europe? Do you think Europeans should have a similar responsibility?*

# Review

- The population of many developing countries has a large percentage of young people. Poor families need the working help of their children, especially in old age.
- The birth rate depends on a number of factors, as diagram D shows.
- As a result of improved health care, people in most parts of the world are now living longer. In Europe, population growth has nearly stopped because people have small families. This has resulted in a larger proportion of older people.

## Children in India are getting a better deal

▲ **E** *Charities now offer ragpickers a new lifestyle*

Sampangi no longer lives on the street. He lives in a hostel run by the Rag-pickers' Educational Development (RED). The hostel provides shelter, security, meals, and education for street children. RED has persuaded local companies to send their waste directly to the shelter so the children don't need to go out on to the streets.

In Madras, hundreds of children now scour the streets with two bags – one for waste and the other for material that can be recycled. The city authorities pay them 800 rupees (£16) a month for cleaning the streets. Added to their money from recycling, this is a good income.

▼ **D** *Factors influencing the birth rate*

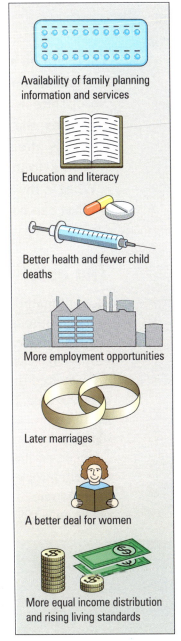

Availability of family planning information and services

Education and literacy

Better health and fewer child deaths

More employment opportunities

Later marriages

A better deal for women

More equal income distribution and rising living standards

**5** Use diagram D to make a list of the factors that help reduce the birth rate. From what you have learned in this unit, which do you think are the most important? Explain your answer.

**6** Work in pairs. One of you chooses the UK, the other India.
   **a)** Try to summarize for each other what you have learned about the populations of these countries.
   **b)** Now team up with another pair. Swap ideas.
   **c)** Still working in a group of four, produce a wall display on the issues facing either youthful or ageing populations. Try to emphasize positive things, for example how young and old contribute to society.

# 2 The active Earth

There are no active volcanoes in the UK today. There is an occasional small earthquake, such as the Clun earthquake in Shropshire in April 1990 which damaged some buildings. In other countries, the natural hazards of volcanoes and earthquakes regularly affect millions of people.

• Where do they occur and why do they happen?
• What is the link between earthquakes and volcanoes?
• What can be done to reduce their effects?

## The eruption of Mount Pinatubo

Mount Pinatubo in the Philippines is not far from the capital city, Manila. Although it had not erupted for 600 years, in 1991 local scientists became worried. They began to record a number of small earthquakes which seemed to be coming from under the mountain. They alerted the US Geological Survey, who set up **seismometers** all over the area. Seismometers are sensitive instruments that record **earth tremors**, the vibrations that are caused by the energy from earthquakes.

It seemed that the earthquakes were caused by the movement of molten rock beneath the mountain. The geologists decided to warn local people to leave their homes. The first eruption of Pinatubo began on 12 June 1991. Three days later there was a massive explosion.

▲ **A** *The location of Mount Pinatubo*

◀ **B** *The eruption of Mount Pinatubo*

**1 a)** Use map A. How far is each of the following from Mount Pinatubo?
(i) Clark Air Force Base
(ii) Subic Bay Naval Base
(iii) Manila

**b)** Read storyboard C. Which of these places was within the area that had to be evacuated?

▲ **C** *Timetable of an eruption*

**2 a)** What were the warning signs that the volcano might erupt?
**b)** Why was it important to try to predict when the eruption might happen?
**c)** The US army and navy did not leave their bases until 13 June. Why do you think they were reluctant to leave the area?

**3** A **typhoon** (tropical storm) hit the area soon after the main eruption. It brought strong winds and heavy rains. Imagine you were one of the last scientists to leave the area on 15 June. Describe how you felt as you left the safety of your building.

**Factfile: Mount Pinatubo**

The eruption of Mount Pinatubo was the biggest since that of Mount Katmai in Alaska, USA, in 1912. Between 5–8km³ of ash were deposited. Ash was blown 30km into the air and covered an area of 80km radius. In some valleys the ash was 200m thick.

## How did it happen?

The molten rock, called **magma**, contained a lot of gas. When the magma reached the surface it began to turn into solid rock although it was still at 700°C. This rock formed a small dome. Finally the pressure from the gas blew the top off the mountain, sending ash clouds high into the air and **pyroclastic flows** of red hot ash down the mountain at speeds of 150kph.

# 'Quake toll nightmare

Japan's nightmare of a major urban earthquake came true today when a powerful tremor tore through central cities, killing more than 1000 people and injuring thousands.

"I thought it was the end of the world," said 64-year-old Minoru Takasu, whose house fell down around him. "I survived by sliding into a small gap between a dish cabinet and the wall," he said. The tragedy shattered Japan's belief that its newer buildings and roads would be able to withstand a major 'quake because of sophisticated engineering.

▲ **D** *Extract from* The Shropshire Star, *17 January 1995*

# Port city reduced to rubble and ashes

Amid the debris, fires fuelled by gas roared from shattered mains while thousands of residents, made homeless by the disaster, huddled around small bonfires in freezing temperatures. Officials said there was ample room for the homeless in government buildings, such as sports halls and schools, but many residents said such facilities were packed. Furniture destroyed in the earthquake was used as firewood. Older people developed hypothermia [extreme cold] and had to be carried off in makeshift ambulances.

▲ **E** *Extract from the* Daily Telegraph, *19 January 1995*

| 17 Jan | 1247 |
| 18 Jan | 1800 |
| 19 Jan | 3021 |
| 21 Jan | 4412 |
| 30 Jan | 5100 |
| 18 Feb | 5390 |

▲ **F** *The rising death toll*

## The economic impact of the earthquake

Kobe's port, which handles more than 12 per cent of Japan's exports, closed except for emergency use. Matsushita, the world's largest manufacturer of consumer electronics, best known for its National and Panasonic brands, stopped production at its Kobe plant. Kobe Steels, one of Japan's biggest steel makers, and the large Sumitomo tyre factory also closed. Over 100 companies reported earthquake damage, which was estimated at US $10.4 billion. Other businesses took advantage of the tragedy. One company increased the cost of roof tiles from 300 yen (£2) each to 5000 yen (£33).

### Factfile: Kobe earthquake

- The earthquake struck Kobe at 5.46 a.m. on 17 January 1995. It measured 7.2 on the Richter scale.
- 5390 people were killed, 656 missing, and 23 600 people were injured.
- More than 40 800 buildings were destroyed or badly damaged.
- 849 500 houses lost their gas supply.

**1 a)** Explain why the death toll at Kobe might have been higher if the earthquake had struck between 7 a.m. and 9 a.m.

**b)** Describe and explain the main cause of death from the earthquake.

**c)** Why were elderly people particularly at risk after the earthquake?

**d)** Suggest two different reasons why the death toll continued to rise for a long time after the earthquake.

**2** Many survivors were critical of the emergency services.

**a)** Explain why the fire brigade and ambulance crews had problems after the earthquake.

**b)** Read extract D again. Why did the earthquake shatter Japan's belief in earthquake engineering?

**3** Describe and explain the impact of the earthquake on the Japanese economy.

**4 a)** How might the Japanese make better preparations for a future earthquake like the one at Kobe?

**b)** *To what extent do you think it is possible to plan for an emergency of this scale?*

# High tech industry: the electronics revolution

Japan is the world's largest producer of the semi-conductors (microchips) that are used in electrical goods such as computers, in defence equipment, and in aircraft. However, the Japanese firms which make TVs and VCRs are making fewer products in Japan than they were in the mid-1980s. Japan is no longer the biggest producer of TVs in the world (it has been overtaken by China) and the third graph in C shows that Japan now imports more TVs than it exports. The reasons for this decline are:

- the home market is dwindling. Most Japanese now own a TV, and 73 per cent own a VCR
- Japanese products are becoming more and more expensive abroad, because the yen is a very strong currency
- TVs and VCRs can be produced more cheaply in other Asian countries such as China and Malaysia, where labour costs are lower than in Japan.

▲ **B** *Microchip factory, Osaka*

► **C** *Japan's changing electronics industry*

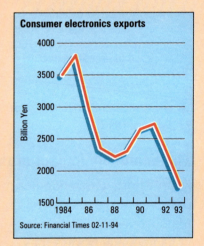
Consumer electronics exports

Source: Financial Times 02-11-94

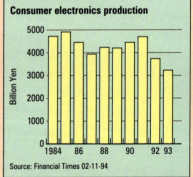
Consumer electronics production

Source: Financial Times 02-11-94

▼ **A** *The location of Japan's electronics plants*

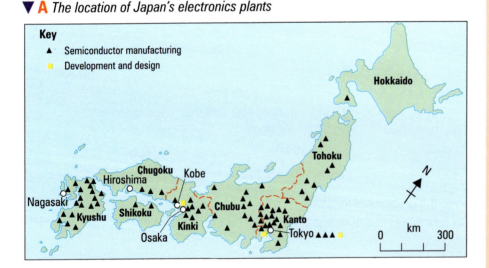

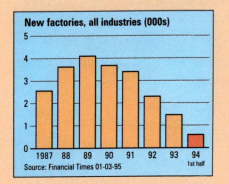
New factories, all industries (000s)
Source: Financial Times 01-03-95

Foreign direct investment by manufacturing companies (accumulated total, US $bn)
Source: Financial Times 01-03-95

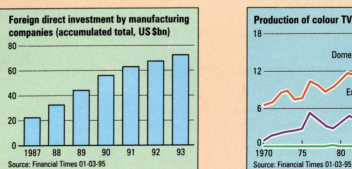
Production of colour TVs (millions)
Source: Financial Times 01-03-95

To keep costs down, many leading Japanese electronics firms have moved their production of TVs and VCRs abroad. The proportion of Japanese goods produced abroad is expected to rise from 16.1 per cent in 1993 to 21.6 per cent in 1997. Not only can the products be made more cheaply, it will also be easier to sell foreign-made products abroad.

## Technological change

The other change in the electronics industry is the research and development of new products. Japanese firms are using their skills to develop products which use new technologies, such as liquid crystal displays and wide screen TVs. Few foreign firms are producing these goods at present and they are difficult to produce overseas because of the high levels of skill required. Sega, Nintendo, Sony and other games companies have recently been redeveloping their hardware too. New machines playing CD-based games are replacing the cartridge consoles used in the early 1990s. CDs are much cheaper to manufacture than cartridges, and also store much more information. Changing to CDs gives customers better games, and gives the games companies bigger profits.

> Labour costs in Japan have become the highest in the world because of the yen's rise. Apart from interest rates, all operating costs, such as the cost of manufacturing sites, construction, water, electricity, and shipping, are also the highest in the world.

*Mr Harus Tsuji, President of Sharp*

> Technology is being shifted overseas and we are worried about the loss of simple assembly skills.

*Mr Minoru Saitoh, local government spokesperson*

▲ **D** *Opinions on Japan's electronics industry in 1995*

◀ **E** *Where your money goes when you buy a computer game (%)*

|  | Publishing | Manufacturing | Distribution and marketing | Retailer |
|---|---|---|---|---|
| PC/CD-ROM | 37 | 8 | 15 | 40 |
| Console cartridge | 10 | 35 | 20 | 35 |

**1 a)** Study map A and describe the location of the electronics industry.
  **b)** Suggest a reason for the location of the development and design plants.

**2** Use the graphs in C and the opinions in D to write a report on the effects of the recent changes in the electronics industry. Include in your report:
  **a)** reasons why the amount of investment in Japan is falling
  **b)** the impact this might have on the economy and workers
  **c)** a description of the rise in investment in foreign plants
  **d)** what you think might happen in the future to this important industry.

**3 a)** Use the data in table E to draw a pair of pie charts.
  **b)** Give two reasons to explain why the electronic games industry is changing the technology of its products.

## Did you know?

The Japanese games company, Sega, is hoping to build Europe's first virtual reality theme park, in Piccadilly Circus, London. Sega, producer of Sonic the Hedgehog, is the world leader in large electronic games and rides. It already has a theme park, Joypolis in Yokohama, Japan, which attracts 1.5 million visitors each year. Here you can experience virtual reality, try space-flight simulators, and ride about in armoured bumper cars.

# The Japanese people and their society

Japan's economy is based on the success of three industries: iron and steel, cars, and high tech industries such as electronics. As in other developed countries, Japan now has more people working in service industries than in manufacturing, as graph A shows. There is little sexual equality: men usually have the best-paid jobs. The Japanese expect to work long hours; many people work ten to thirteen hours every day. They often work on Saturday and Sunday as well. Bank staff often work from 7 a.m. to 11 p.m. and then they are expected to have a drink with their boss. The Japanese system demands that employees stay at work until the boss goes home.

Workers want to appear loyal and hard-working. They won't take all their holiday allowance if the boss doesn't take his. Lawyers estimate that 10 000 Japanese (both male and female) die every year through overwork. Every year about 500 families take the companies of their dead relatives to court, claiming they were killed by overwork. Few of them succeed.

School in Japan is quite different from that in our system. Much learning is done by rote (repetition), and pupils are not asked to form opinions of their own. Japanese children take regular tests and examinations, in a system known as *shiken jigoku*, 'examination hell'. They even have entrance exams for infant classes. Getting into university is also difficult, but once there life is easier. 'The university does not require you to work, and many students hardly ever open a book,' according to one Japanese student.

▼ **A** *Percentage of the work force employed*

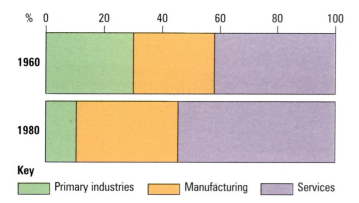

**Key**

☐ Primary industries ☐ Manufacturing ☐ Services

▼ **B** *Rock and roll fans in Yoyogi Park*

**1 a)** Describe how Japan's employment changed between 1960 and 1980.
**b)** Use the following figures to plot your own divided bar of employment in Japan today:
- primary industries 7%
- manufacturing 33%
- services 60%.
**c)** What trend is shown by the three graphs?

**2 a)** Describe the kind of problems that might occur for employees and their families as a result of the Japanese attitude to work.
**b)** Suggest how Japanese working conditions could be improved.

**3** Suggest reasons why some employers are becoming critical of the Japanese education system.

**4** Look at graph C.
  **a)** By how much did the percentage of people over 65 increase between 1950 and 1988?
  **b)** By how much will the percentage of people over 65 increase between 1988 and 2040? (Express your answer as a multiple, such as ×2 or ×3.)
  **c)** Why is the 15–64 age group labelled as the 'productive' part of the population?
  **d)** Describe carefully the change that the 15–64 age group has already gone through, and how it is predicted to change in the future.

**5** Use graph D.
  **a)** Which country currently has the highest proportion of people aged over 65?
  **b)** Compare the trend of the lines for the UK and Japan.
  **c)** Why are some Japanese beginning to worry about the future population structure of the country?

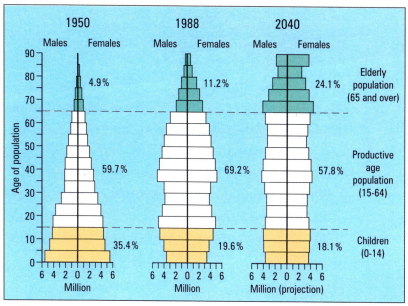

▲ **C** *The ageing Japanese population*

As you can see from graphs C and D, Japan has an ageing population. After the Second World War the Japanese government were worried that the rise in population would divert money needed for economic growth into housing, education, and welfare projects. Consequently, family planning and birth control were encouraged in the early 1950s, and abortion was legalized. The birth rate began to fall. As Japanese families became wealthier during the 1960s and 1970s, the birth rate dropped further. People tended to marry later in life and have smaller families. This trend is linked to the high cost of living, especially the high cost of housing.

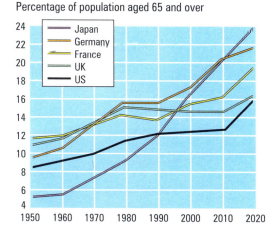

▲ **D** *Population structure*

## Review

Japan's mountainous terrain means that most people live on the coastal plains, in huge conurbations. There is a constant threat of volcanic eruptions and earthquakes because of the movement of crustal plates. Japan has tried to use its wealth and technology to overcome these hazards, but the Kobe earthquake on 17 January 1995 proved that some disasters cannot be avoided.

  The Japanese people work very hard and have helped to build a successful economy, but the ageing population and high labour costs are worrying the economists. Japan is at the forefront of world technology, but it lags behind other countries on green issues such as whaling and rainforest depletion.

# **5** *Energy*

We use energy to heat and light our homes, cook our food, provide power in our factories, and for transport. In this unit we will be asking:
- what resources are used to make energy?
- what impacts do different forms of energy have on the environment?
- how can we conserve energy or use energy more efficiently?

## Using energy

Think for a moment – how long after you wake up do you switch on something that uses electricity? Five minutes? Half an hour? Can you imagine a day spent without using electricity or gas? Our lives all depend on them. Each day you are likely to use six times more energy than someone living in China, and sixteen times more energy than someone living in India. Not only do we use a lot of energy, we waste it by using it inefficiently – up to 65 per cent of the energy we produce is lost or wasted. Diagram A shows how little of the energy from coal actually provides light in a normal light bulb.

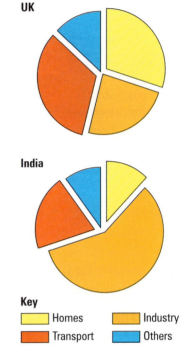

**UK**

**India**

**Key**
- Homes
- Industry
- Transport
- Others

▲ **B** *Energy use in the UK and India (1990)*

▼ **A** *From coal to electric light*

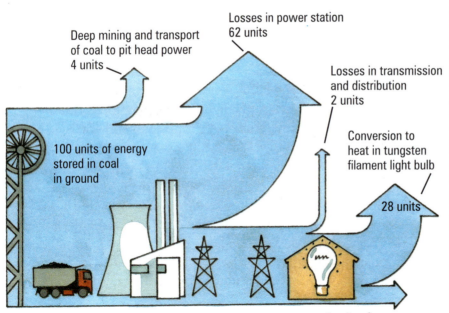

Deep mining and transport of coal to pit head power
4 units

Losses in power station
62 units

Losses in transmission and distribution
2 units

Conversion to heat in tungsten filament light bulb

28 units

100 units of energy stored in coal in ground

4 units of energy as light from light bulb

1 List all the things you use in an average day that use energy. Split the list into things that you regard as essential, and things that could be seen as luxuries. Is there anything you could use less energy for? Is there anything you are prepared to do without?

2 Study diagram A.
   a) Where is most energy lost?
   b) How much energy is lost from the light bulb?
   c) What percentage of the energy in the coal is used by the light bulb?
   d) How might less coal be used to provide the same amount of light?

## Fossil fuels

Energy from the **fossil fuels** oil, gas, and coal is used to generate 90 per cent of electricity in the UK. There are limited supplies of fossil fuels, and once they are gone they cannot be replaced for many thousands of years. For this reason, fossil fuels are also called non-renewables. Map D shows how long different **fuel reserves** will last if we continue to use fuel at the rate we use it today.

▼ **C** *UK energy use 1960–1993*

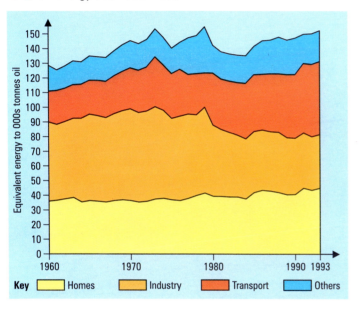

Key: Homes | Industry | Transport | Others

**3** Use the information in diagrams B and C.
  **a)** How is India's use of energy different from that of the UK?
  **b)** Describe how our use of energy in the UK is changing.

**4** Using map D, name the areas of the world you think are rich in fuel reserves and those you think have poor fuel reserves. Give reasons for your answers.

**5 a)** *Do we all use the same amount of energy? Use this table to help you.*

| Country | % of world population | % of energy consumed |
|---|---|---|
| USA | 4 | 24 |
| India | 16 | 2 |
| China | 22 | 8 |

**b)** *Do people in the West always use energy wisely? Look back at your answer to question 1. Explain why we should consider how energy is used.*

▼ **D** *World reserves of fossil fuels. The bars are proportional to the amount of fuel left*

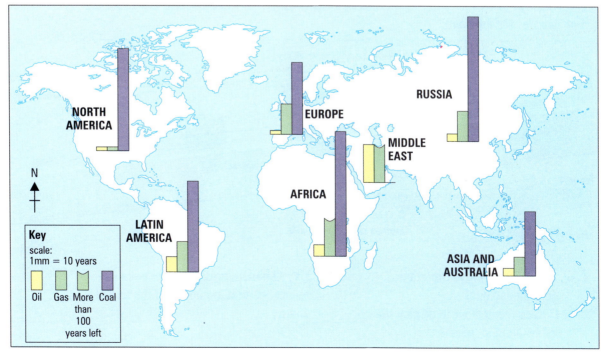

# Energy and the environment

All forms of energy have some impact on the environment. What are the impacts of burning fossil fuels? The Sun's energy passes through the atmosphere and warms the surface of the Earth. Heat is both reflected and radiated from the Earth. This heat is trapped by carbon dioxide ($CO_2$) and other greenhouse gases in the atmosphere. This is known as the **greenhouse effect**. A certain amount of such warming is essential. Without it, scientists believe, the atmosphere would be on average 33°C colder than it is.

## Global warming

The amount of greenhouse gases is increasing. Burning fossil fuels and wood releases more and more $CO_2$ into the atmosphere. Other gas emissions from industry, vehicles, and farming add to the amount of 'greenhouse gases' in the atmosphere. Some scientists believe this will lead to a rise in average global temperature over the next century. Ice caps could begin to melt, and areas on the edges of deserts could become hotter and drier.

▶ **A** *How pollution increases the greenhouse effect and leads to global warming*

▼ **B** *Global warming: the greenhouse gases*

| Carbon dioxide | 50% |
|---|---|
| CFCs | 14% |
| Methane | 18% |
| Nitrous oxide | 6% |
| Surface ozone | 12% |

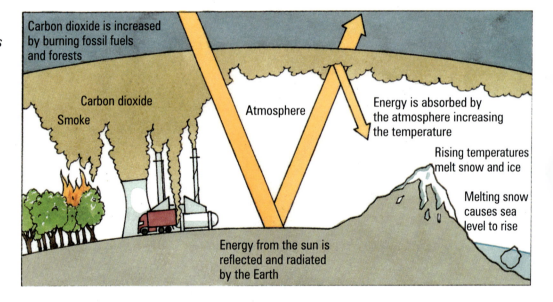

Carbon dioxide is increased by burning fossil fuels and forests

Carbon dioxide

Smoke

Atmosphere

Energy is absorbed by the atmosphere increasing the temperature

Rising temperatures melt snow and ice

Melting snow causes sea level to rise

Energy from the sun is reflected and radiated by the Earth

▼ **C** *Sources of CFCs, carbon dioxide, and methane*

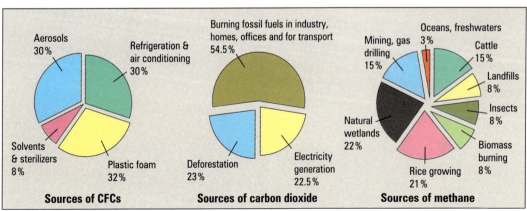

Aerosols 30%

Refrigeration & air conditioning 30%

Solvents & sterilizers 8%

Plastic foam 32%

**Sources of CFCs**

Burning fossil fuels in industry, homes, offices and for transport 54.5%

Natural wetlands 22%

Deforestation 23%

Electricity generation 22.5%

**Sources of carbon dioxide**

Mining, gas drilling 15%

Oceans, freshwaters 3%

Cattle 15%

Landfills 8%

Insects 8%

Biomass burning 8%

Rice growing 21%

**Sources of methane**

▼ **D** *Estimated impact of **global warming** on sea levels*

| Predicted sea level rise (figures in cm) | | |
|---|---|---|
| Year | Best estimate | Worst estimate |
| 2000 | 5 | 8 |
| 2020 | 12 | 20 |
| 2040 | 25 | 40 |
| 2060 | 35 | 60 |
| 2080 | 48 | 85 |
| 2100 | 65 | 110 |

**1 a)** Which is the most important greenhouse gas?

**b)** Draw a divided bar to display the information in table B.

**2** List all the sources of greenhouse gas emissions that are linked to the use of energy.

Increasing greenhouse gases will affect the world's climate. Temperatures will rise, and storms may become more common. In hot, dry regions of the world droughts and food shortages might happen more often. Map E shows one forecast of changes in temperature around the world. Table D shows that sea levels will rise, but it is difficult to predict by how much.

▼ **E** *How temperatures in different parts of the world will be affected*

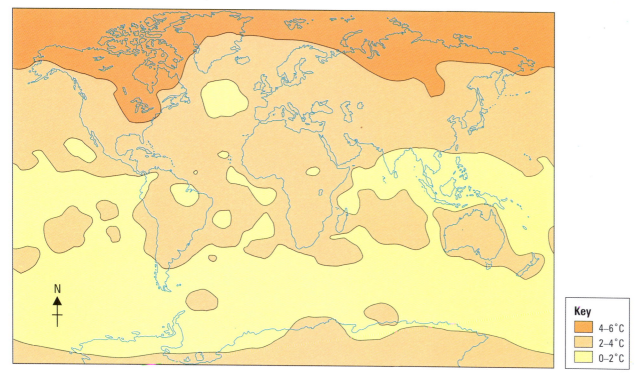

**Key**
- 4–6 °C
- 2–4 °C
- 0–2 °C

**3** Study diagram A. How would rising temperatures lead to a rise in sea level?

**4** Use table D to draw a line graph. Draw two lines to show the best and worst estimates of the increase in sea level.

**5** Use map E.
  **a)** In which part of the world will temperatures rise most?
  **b)** Why is this particularly worrying?
  **c)** By how much will temperatures rise in the desert areas of Africa and north-west India?
  **d)** How might people who live in these arid areas be affected?

**6** Study map F.
  **a)** How far are Cambridge and Norwich from the sea?
  **b)** List the towns that would be flooded.
  **c)** What transport problems would be created by flooding?

▼ **F** *The Fens in East Anglia are under serious threat of flooding*

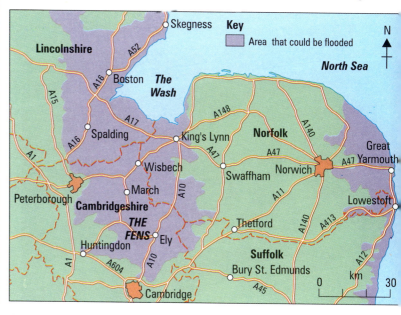

**Key**
- Area that could be flooded

## The threat of coastal flooding

Low-lying coastal areas such as East Anglia in the UK, the Netherlands, and Bangladesh would be badly affected by even a small rise in sea level. Coral islands such as the Seychelles in the Indian Ocean could be completely submerged. A rise of only 45cm would submerge 70 per cent of the Seychelles. Pacific islanders are also extremely worried about possible flooding. The tiny island of Tuvalu is one island under threat. It has an area of 16km$^2$ and a population of 9000. Average incomes are below US $700 per year.

▼ **A** *The island of Tuvalu in the Pacific Ocean*

◀**B** *Extract from* The Independent, *1 November 1992*

## Why is tiny Tuvalu getting so annoyed with Britain?

Tuvalu as a country may cease to exist next century if the Earth gets warmer. Its highest point is one metre above sea level, and storms in the Pacific Ocean are already washing over the country. The European Union is building a sea barrier of four-legged concrete blocks to protect the capital, Foangafale. And the Dutch said that they would look into the possibility of a sea wall. Only Britain seems to want to stand apart.

▶ **C** *Aerial view of Tarawa, Kiribati, South Pacific, an island similar to Tuvalu*

▼ **D** *Sea wall protecting a Pacific island*

**1 a)** In what two ways is Tuvalu at risk from global warming?

**b)** Use table D on page 52 to predict when Tuvalu will be submerged by the sea.

**2** Why is tiny Tuvalu getting so annoyed with Britain?

**3** Explain how the sea defences have been built in photo D. Who do you think should be responsible for this work? Give reasons for your answer.

## Coastal defences in the Netherlands

The Netherlands is a rich European country with an average income of US $20 590. Its best farm land, the **polders**, was reclaimed from the sea and these fields are already below sea level, as map F shows. Of the 15.4 million people who live in the Netherlands, 9 million live in the polders.

The Dutch people have built an expensive system of sea defences. Granite boulders imported from Germany are dumped offshore to break the force of the waves. Large concrete blocks are also used. A **dyke** (embankment) prevents the sea from flooding the polders. Rock **groynes** help to trap beach material in front of the dyke. Barrages built across the mouths of rivers help prevent flooding of the estuaries at high tide.

▲ **E** *Oosterschelde flood prevention barrage, the Netherlands*

▼ **F** *The low-lying areas of the Netherlands*

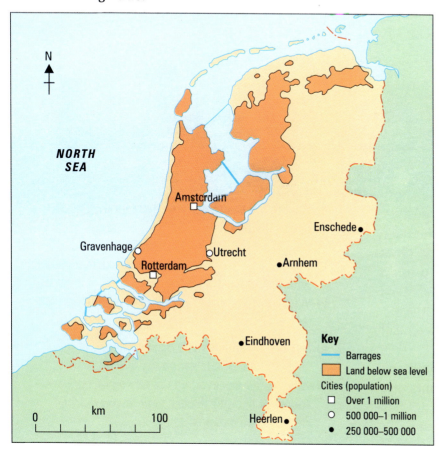

N

NORTH SEA

Amsterdam

Enschede

Gravenhage
Utrecht
Rotterdam
Arnhem

Eindhoven

**Key**
— Barrages
▨ Land below sea level
Cities (population)
□ Over 1 million
○ 500 000–1 million
● 250 000–500 000

Heerlen

0          km          100

**4 a)** List the cities in the Netherlands that are at or below sea level.
**b)** Roughly what percentage of the Netherlands is at risk from flooding?

**5** Using map F, and the text, produce a labelled diagram to show how the polders are defended against coastal flooding.

**6 a)** Make two lists, one of similarities, one of differences, between Tuvalu and the Netherlands.
**b)** How could the Dutch people help Tuvalu?

**7** *Write a report on global warming. Explain:*
*a) why it is happening*
*b) what its effects may be*
*c) why the people who suffer the effects of sea level rise might feel angry with developed nations such as the UK and USA.*

# Nuclear power

At present the UK gets most of its energy from the three fossil fuels – coal, oil, and gas. The best developed alternative is nuclear power. However, several countries are looking at reducing their nuclear programmes. The USA, for example, has stopped building nuclear power stations. In the UK the government is reviewing the development of nuclear power. Why are countries having second thoughts about nuclear power? Do the problems of nuclear power really outweigh the benefits?

## Power generation in France

France has very rapidly created the most developed nuclear industry in the world. **Nuclear power** provides 75 per cent of France's electricity from 56 nuclear reactors. France has very small reserves of oil, coal, and gas, so the development of nuclear power has greatly reduced its dependence on fuel imports from other countries. Its carbon dioxide emissions are among the lowest in Europe. The cost of developing the nuclear power industry has been very high; Electricité de France (EdF), the state electricity company, had a debt of £25.4 billion by 1990.

▼ **A** *Nuclear power production in France and the UK*

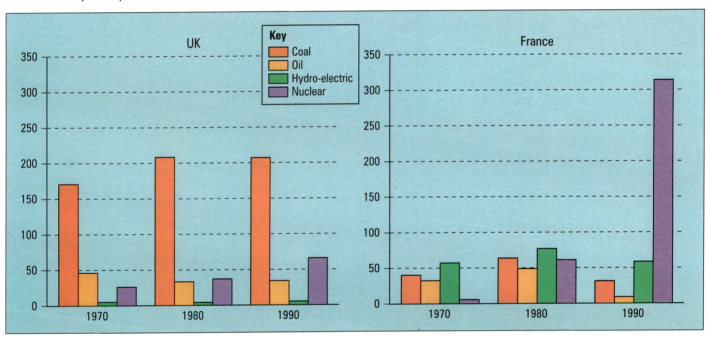

## Problems of nuclear power in France

France relies heavily on nuclear power as its major form of electricity generation, and this has caused problems. During 1989–1990 design faults were found in several nuclear reactors. At the same time a major drought affected the supply of water to some nuclear plants. The drought also affected the country's **hydro-electric** schemes. Together these factors greatly reduced the power supply. As a result France had to import electricity.

The nuclear programme has also caused problems for the environment. It produces large amounts of radioactive waste but the industry still does not have an accepted way of dealing with the waste safely.

1 Use graph A.
   a) How much electricity was generated by nuclear power in France in
      (i) 1970   (ii) 1980   (iii) 1990?
   b) Compare France's development of nuclear power with that of the UK.
   c) Which form of electricity generation does the UK rely on?

2 a) List the advantages and disadvantages of the development of nuclear power in France.
   b) What is the disadvantage of relying on only one source of energy? Explain your answer using France as an example.

## International problems

In April 1986 an accident at Chernobyl in Ukraine had a massive impact on people and the environment. An explosion in one reactor blew a large amount of radioactive material 5km into the atmosphere. This then spread across Europe, from Scandinavia to Greece. High levels of radioactivity were found as far away as the UK. Soldiers who tried to stop the leak died. Local people were evacuated, and some have become sick. Soil, plants, and animals were contaminated as far away as northern Scandinavia and north Wales. European countries are now worried about the safety of the remaining reactors in Russia and eastern Europe.

▲ **B** *The damaged nuclear reactor at Chernobyl*

**Factfile: Chernobyl**

- 31 people died immediately, others are now dying from illnesses caused by the high levels of **radiation**
- 10 000km² land was contaminated
- 220 villages were abandoned
- In 600 villages soldiers tried to decontaminate buildings
- 116 000 people were evacuated and 500 000 made homeless

▼ **C** *Opinion of Austrian Environment Minister*

We decided in the late 1970s not to develop a nuclear programme. But we have become increasingly concerned about the reactors close to our border in the Czech Republic and Slovakia. So much so that we have offered the Czech Republic free electricity if it will shut down some of its closest, older reactors. We call on our neighbours to help widen the 'nuclear free zone' within central Europe.

▲ **D** *Nuclear plants in the Czech Republic and Slovakia*

**3 a)** List the problems caused by the explosion at Chernobyl.

  **b)** Use an atlas to find how far it is from northern Sweden to Greece.

  **c)** Why is nuclear power an international issue?

**4** Using the information on this page, explain why the Austrian Minister in C is concerned about the nuclear reactors in the Czech Republic and Slovakia.

**5 a)** *Identify the factors that should be considered when comparing environmental impacts of different energy programmes. The following headings should start you off:*

  **Type of pollution**    **Impact on people**

  **b)** *Explain why each factor needs to be considered, using examples from the book.*

# Renewable energy

**Renewable energy** is generated from sources which are constantly being replaced, such as the wind, sun, and water. The energy from renewable sources used during 1993 in the UK was just under 1 per cent of all the energy used. Many experts think we could produce far more renewable energy. Some people believe that renewables could produce 20 per cent of our electricity supply by 2005.

There has been a great deal of interest in wind power in the UK. Wind generators create no waste and no greenhouse gases; besides, the wind is free and cannot be used up. But even renewable forms of energy cause problems. Each wind generator produces a relatively small amount of electricity, and so between 25 000 and 35 000 wind generators would be needed to produce 20 per cent of the UK's electricity. People think that this number of wind turbines would look ugly, make too much noise, and interfere with TV pictures. Yet this number of wind generators is smaller than the 50 000 electricity pylons already sited around the country. We accept that if we want electricity at the flick of a switch we must have pylons.

▼ **A** *Small-scale hydro-electric power station near Wan-Xian, China*

## Factfile: Renewable energy

- Wind – wind turbines can be used to generate electricity or pump water.
- Sun – solar panels absorb energy from the sun and either heat water or generate electricity.
- Water – water flows through a turbine, generating electricity. This is known as hydro-electric power (HEP). A small-scale example is shown in photo A and diagram B.
- Sea power – energy could be generated from the rising and falling of the waves. Barrages (or dams) built across an estuary could generate electricity from the movement of the tides.
- Geothermal energy – water is pumped down deep holes in the ground to extract heat from hot rocks in the Earth's crust (see page 23).
- Energy from waste – the waste that we produce can be burnt to produce heat or electricity. Methane (biogas) from rotting waste or sewage can be burnt to produce heat and generate electricity.

**1 a)** List the renewable energy sources that are dependent on climatic conditions.

**b)** Find the UK and Zimbabwe in an atlas. Suggest how the two countries might benefit from different renewable sources of energy. Give reasons for your answers.

**2** Make a sketch of photo A. Use diagram B to label it.

▼ **B** *How a small-scale hydro-electric power station works*

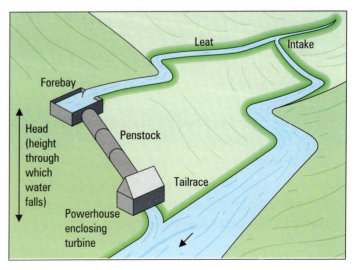

**3 a)** List the advantages and disadvantages of wind farms.
  **b)** Would you prefer a wind farm or coal-fired power station near your home? What problems might each cause?

## Energy from waste

In 1994, of all the household waste in the UK, 87 per cent was tipped on **landfill** sites. These sites can cause serious environmental problems, as diagram D shows. Instead of throwing our rubbish away, we could use it to generate electricity.

● Domestic, industrial, or agricultural waste can be burnt to produce energy in the form of hot water or electricity.

● Methane (biogas) is produced when material decomposes (rots) without oxygen. The gas can be produced from landfill sites, sewage works, and farm slurry. Methane can then be burnt to produce heat and generate electricity.

Biogas has been used a lot in developing countries. The production of biogas involves the whole community in a far greater way than energy production in the UK.

  The people of Gujarat in India used to cook using firewood. But deforestation was causing serious problems, and women were walking further and further to collect wood. Biogas plants have been set up to provide energy in some villages. One such plant is in Methan, Gujarat. Sources A to E on the next page explain how the biogas scheme works and how it is run by local people.

▲ **C** *Waste leaching from this landfill site is carried by the ditch into a tank*

| Landfill | 83% |
|---|---|
| Incineration (burning) | 7% |
| Recycling | 5% |
| Landfill producing biogas | 3% |
| Incineration producing energy | 2% |

▲ **E** *Disposal of UK household waste*

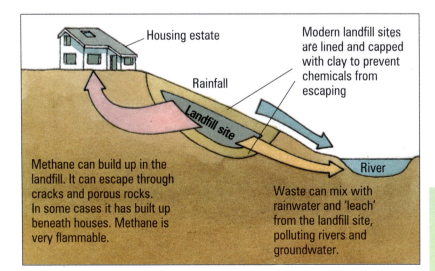

Housing estate

Rainfall

Modern landfill sites are lined and capped with clay to prevent chemicals from escaping

Landfill site

River

Methane can build up in the landfill. It can escape through cracks and porous rocks. In some cases it has built up beneath houses. Methane is very flammable.

Waste can mix with rainwater and 'leach' from the landfill site, polluting rivers and groundwater.

▲ **D** *The possible environmental hazards of landfill sites*

**4** Describe two problems caused by landfill sites.

**5 a)** Use table E to draw a graph of UK domestic waste disposal.
  **b)** How could our waste disposal be improved?

# The biogas co-operative scheme

The biogas plant in Methan, Gujarat, is run by the community. Manure is collected from all the members of the project who have cattle. This manure ferments in the chamber to produce methane gas. This gas is then used for cooking and the solid waste from the biogas chamber is used as fertilizer for the crops. The gas and fertilizer are given to the members in proportion to the amount of manure they provided in the first place.

▲ **B** *Biogas co-operative plant in Methan, India*

▶ **A**

It took a long time to convince people. It was difficult to persuade them to contribute gobar (dung) to the gas plant. They would not believe that slurry from the gas plant is a richer fertilizer, or that they should fit in with the community cooking times. Also, people want to keep taking the wood that is free rather than pay the small sum to become co-operative members.

We have gained so much, especially us women. No more smoky homes, no coughs or burning eyes, for us or for our children who are with us all the time in the kitchen. And how much time we save, not looking for firewood every day!

▼ **C** *Villagers collecting manure from members of the co-operative*

▶ **D** *Cross-section of the biogas plant*

Mixing pit   Gas holder   Gas pipe
Outlet
Ground level
Slurry
Inlet pipe
Partition wall

▼ **E** *Cooking before and after installing biogas*

BEFORE

AFTER

**1** What problems does the use of firewood cause for:
   **a)** women   **b)** the environment?

**2** Briefly describe the stages involved in providing gas to the members of the biogas co-operative.

**3** List the benefits of the scheme for:
   **a)** the villagers   **b)** the environment.

**4** Imagine you were one of the villagers trying to set up the co-operative scheme. What would you say to persuade another villager to join?

**5** What advantages might community biogas schemes have for people in the UK?

# Saving energy and recycling

As well as finding alternative sources of energy, we should also try to find ways of using energy more efficiently. Energy can be saved by avoiding wasteful packaging materials, or by reusing them. Materials can also be recycled. It takes 25 times less electricity to recycle an aluminium drinks can than to make a new one.

Energy can also be conserved around the house. Using long-life, low-energy light bulbs is one example. Image F shows how much energy is lost from an average family house. Diagram G shows how this can be improved. Houses are now being designed and built to be as **energy efficient** as possible. Photo H shows one such house. The front has large windows (top picture); while the back has small windows (bottom picture).

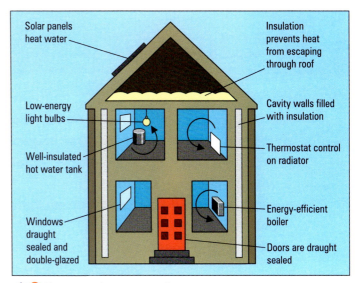

▲ **G** *How to reduce energy loss*

▲ **F** *Typical energy loss from a family house – red shows the warmest areas (greatest heat loss), blue the coolest areas (greatest insulation)*

▲ **H** *Energy-efficient house, front and back*

**6** Look at diagram G, and photos F and H.
   **a)** Where is most energy lost from the house?
   **b)** Photo H shows both sides of the same house. Which side do you think faces south? Why?
   **c)** The house in photo H is an energy-efficient house. What other things do you think it might have to save energy?

**7 a)** What energy-saving improvements could be made to your school buildings?
   **b)** Write an energy-saving policy for your school.

## Review

Energy is an essential resource but it is not shared equally. As the fossil fuels are being used up, we must look for alternative sources of energy. In making decisions about energy production we need to consider:
- what impact it might have on the environment
- how we can use energy more efficiently.

# 6 Superdams

Many countries build massive dams. They are used to control rivers and provide water for huge irrigation projects. This unit looks at two huge schemes where 'superdams' are being built:

- why do people build superdams?
- what impacts do superdam projects have on local people and the environment?
- why do some people think that small-scale projects are better?

GHANA

## Why do we need superdams?

After heavy rain, some rivers flood, causing loss of life and damage to property. By building a dam, flood water can be captured while the river flow is high. Water can then be released when the danger of flooding has passed. Dams can therefore control flooding. They are also used to:

- generate hydro-electric power, a clean and renewable form of energy
- supply water for homes, industry, and agriculture.

The Hoover Dam in the USA was the world's first **superdam**. Since then, there have been many superdam projects. Many have been in developing countries.

▲ **A** The Akosombo Dam

### Akosombo – an early superdam

One of the first superdams to be built in the developing world was on the River Volta in Ghana. The dam was completed in 1964 at a cost of US $120 million. Its aim was to produce the huge quantities of hydro-electric power needed to smelt bauxite, the **ore** of aluminium. The aluminium smelter at the port of Tema uses 70 per cent of the electricity produced by the dam. Most of Ghana's aluminium is exported to the USA by the American company who own the plant.

**1 a)** Use the data in B to draw bar graphs of superdams under construction. You could cut out and paste your bars on to a world map.

**b)** In which parts of the world are most of the new superdams being built – in developed or developing countries?

| Location | No. |
|---|---|
| Canada | 1 |
| Latin America | 17 |
| China | 7 |
| East and south-east Asia | 8 |
| Turkey | 1 |
| India | 4 |
| Europe | 4 |
| USSR | 2 |
| Africa | 4 |

▲ **B** Superdam projects under construction, 1990

## The effects of the Akosombo dam

- 99% of Ghana's electricity is produced by the dam. Surplus electricity is exported to Togo, Benin, and Ivory Coast, earning foreign exchange for Ghana.
- Water from Lake Volta is used to irrigate the dry savanna landscape to the north of the dam.
- A large fishing industry has grown up on Lake Volta.

Since the completion of the dam, coastal erosion in parts of Ghana and Togo has become more rapid.

- Most of Keta, in Ghana, has fallen into the sea.
- Coast roads in Togo have been washed away.
- Rock groynes could be built to protect the coast, but would cost around US $2–3 million per kilometre of coastline.

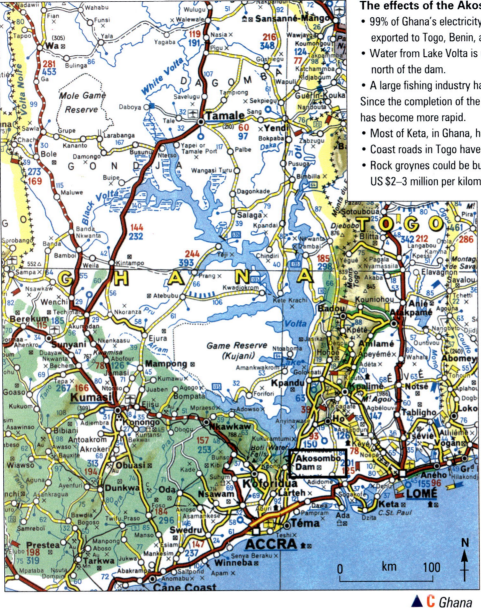

▲ **C** *Ghana*

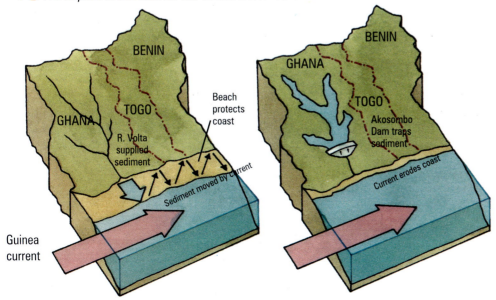

▼ **D** *The impact of the dam on the West African coast*

2 Using map C, copy and complete the following sentences:
The main tributaries of Lake Volta are the ....... Volta in the north-west, the White Volta in the ......., and the ....... in the north-east. Lake Volta is ....... km long from Tamale to the dam at ........

3 Study diagram D.
 a) In which direction does the Guinea current flow?
 b) Explain in your own words how the construction of the dam is linked to problems of coastal erosion.
 c) Use map C to name one town in Ghana and one in Togo that may be affected by erosion.

4 Summarize the advantages and disadvantages of Akosombo Dam for Ghana and its neighbouring countries.

# The Three Gorges Dam in China

The Three Gorges Dam is currently being built on the Yangtze River in China. The Yangtze is the third largest river in the world, with a huge flood plain where 75 million people live. It is a dangerous and unpredictable river. In July 1995, 100 million people were affected by flooding on the Yangtze. One million homes were destroyed and over 1000 people died in the worst floods since 1935. The flooding was caused by torrential rain since May, and the thaw of snow in the mountains at the source of the river. **Deforestation** was also blamed. The floods were used as a powerful argument to complete the Three Gorges Dam. The finished dam will be 175 metres wide, creating a **reservoir** 600km long. The project will cost US $20 billion.

▲ **A** *The dramatic scenery of the gorges on the Yangtze*

**1** Use map B and an atlas to name:
  **a)** the river in northern China that flows into the Yellow Sea
  **b)** the river in southern China that flows into the South China Sea near Hong Kong.

**2 a)** Describe the four aims of the Three Gorges project.

**b)** Imagine you work for the Chinese authorities. Use map B as evidence to explain why the dam is necessary.

**3** The World Bank believes that living standards in China will be improved if electricity production is increased. Suggest how this might happen.

▶ **B**

*Risk of flooding from major Chinese rivers*

**Key**
▮ Severe flooding
▮ Occasional flooding

The main aims of the project are:
* To control the river and prevent flooding. Records show that floods have occurred on average every ten years on the Yangtze River. In 1935 a flood killed 142 000 people and caused extensive damage. The basin of the Yangtze produces 40 per cent of China's total industrial and agricultural output. Reducing the risk of flooding is very important to ensure future economic growth.
* To generate hydro-electric power. The Three Gorges Dam should generate 18 200 megawatts, which is 18 per cent of China's present energy needs.
* To provide a steady flow of water for **irrigation**. More and more rural Chinese are leaving the land to find jobs in China's cities. Since 1980 there has been a steady decline in agriculture. The dam will provide water to improve the livelihood of farmers by allowing them to grow cash crops like flowers, as well as cereals.
* To make river transport easier. At the moment the upper Yangtze flows down a gorge 660km long and drops down 139 rapids. When the reservoir has been filled, the rapids will be flooded to a safe depth. Ships of 10 000 tonnes will be able to travel up the river, cutting transport costs by 35%.

## What are the costs of the dam?

The Three Gorges Dam will flood 632km$^2$ of land, including 240 000 hectares of farm land, and two cities. Over one million people will need to be resettled. The loss of farm land and of people's homes causes a great deal of worry amongst local people. Where will they live and work? Will they be fully compensated for their lost homes and businesses?

## What about the environment?

Some argue that the dramatic scenery of the **gorges** will be ruined when the water levels rise by an average of 40m up the cliff faces.

Conservationists fear that the freshwater dolphin will no longer be able to live in the fast-running water below the dam. Another rare creature, the huge Chinese sturgeon, swims up river to spawn, but its route will be blocked by the dam.

Forest clearance in the area is also causing concern. The pie charts in C show that most of the area has already been deforested. As the dam is built and people are moved to new sites, more trees will be cut down to create farm land, and to provide wood for building and fuel. Once areas of land are left bare and unprotected, **soil erosion** quickly follows, as diagram C shows.

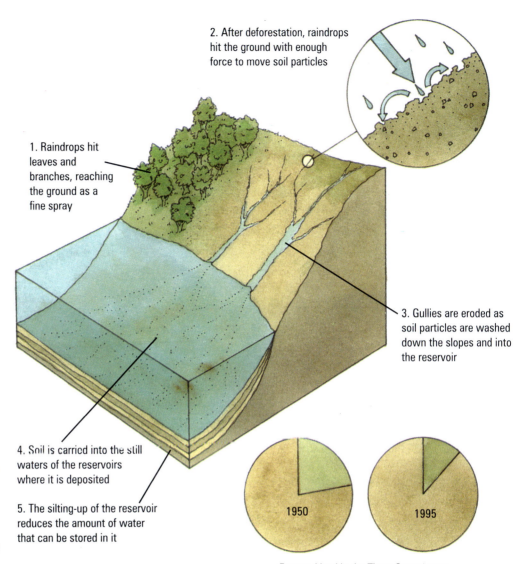

2. After deforestation, raindrops hit the ground with enough force to move soil particles

1. Raindrops hit leaves and branches, reaching the ground as a fine spray

3. Gullies are eroded as soil particles are washed down the slopes and into the reservoir

4. Soil is carried into the still waters of the reservoirs where it is deposited

5. The silting-up of the reservoir reduces the amount of water that can be stored in it

1950    1995

Forested land in the Three Gorges area

▲ C *Some impacts of deforestation*

**4** Imagine that you are either a conservationist or one of the families that will be forced to move to make way for the dam. Write about how you feel.

**5 a)** What percentage of forest was left in the area in 1950 and in 1995?
  **b)** Use diagram C to explain how deforestation can lead to silting-up of the reservoir.
  **c)** Why is silting-up of reservoirs a problem, and how can it be prevented?

**6 a)** Rank the arguments for the dam in order of importance, giving reasons for your order.
  **b)** Do the same for the arguments against the dam.
  **c)** Do you think the advantages outweigh the disadvantages?

# Are there alternatives to superdams?

How can developing countries provide irrigation water and hydro-electric power without causing massive environmental damage or moving thousands of people from their homes?

## Small-scale solutions to water shortage

Adgaon is a village in the Indian state of Maharashtra. It is 240km south of the site of the Sardar Sarovar superdam on the Narmada River. Adgaon receives an average of 500mm of rainfall a year. Most of this rain falls between July and October, much of it in just ten days. The villagers suffer during the rainy season from the effects of unpredictable rainfall, lack of drinking water, and soil erosion.

The villagers have now constructed small earth dams across the streams. This is an example of **appropriate technology**. The earth dams use local materials and the skills of local people. They are cheap to build and easy to maintain. Water is stored for several months during the dry season. Farmers can later dig out the fertile **silt** that has washed down and been trapped behind the dam. They spread the silt on their fields, and it helps keep the land fertile.

The villagers have also built earth walls or ***bunds*** along the contours of fields. These slow down the run-off of rainwater, trapping the water where it falls. This is known as rainwater harvesting. B*unds* also prevent soil erosion. They have been used in other arid areas, such as the Sahel on the edge of the Sahara, as you can see in photo D.

The results in Adgaon are impressive; the wells now have water and there are fish in the main stream, even in December when the river used to be dry. Acacia, eucalyptus, and banana trees have been planted and now thrive in Adgaon.

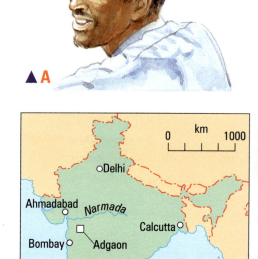

Large-scale schemes which require a lot of money are not an appropriate form of development for developing countries like India. Countries should develop in more sustainable ways that require less money and involve people on a local scale.

▲ **A**

▲ **B** *Location of Adgaon, India*

◄ **C** *A small earth dam in Adgaon village, India*

| Region | Area | Area affected by erosion |
|--------|------|--------------------------|
| North | 150.6 | 40.7 |
| Sahel | 802.4 | 224.0 |
| South | 295.0 | 58.7 |
| Others | 38.0 | 8.9 |
| **Total** | **1286.0** | **332.3** |

▲ **F** *Soil erosion in Africa's regions (millions of hectares)*

▲ **D** *Villagers learning about* bunds. *Full-size* bunds *are longer and about 0.5m high*

Other small-scale methods of water management:
- crops can be grown in hollows that collect rain water around the plant
- hillsides can be terraced to create strips of flat land and reduce soil erosion
- simple, low-cost wells and pumps can tap into groundwater or local streams.

**1** Describe how the rainfall pattern in Adgaon causes problems in the water supply.

**2** Look at photo C. Explain why small earth dams such as this can be more helpful to the local community than a superdam such as the Three Gorges.

**3** Imagine you work for an aid agency in Africa. Describe what *bunds* are to local villagers and explain how they can help conserve water.

**4 a)** Using map E and an atlas, name countries A–D.
   **b)** Using F, draw graphs to show the area affected by soil erosion in each region.
   **c)** Which region has the largest percentage of its area affected?

**5** *Explain why the developments in Adgaon can be described as appropriate.*

**6** Describe the advantages and disadvantages of small scale hydro-electric power schemes compared to large projects like the Three Gorges.

## Small-scale solutions to energy production

In China small hydro-electric power stations (like photo A, page 58) are built by local communities and subsidized by the government. They need less money to build and cause much less damage than superdams although each unit of electricity is slightly more expensive in the long term. They can be maintained and operated by rural communities and integrated to form a local grid. These small-scale schemes are a healthy answer to local power shortages but can only partly meet power generation needs on a large scale.

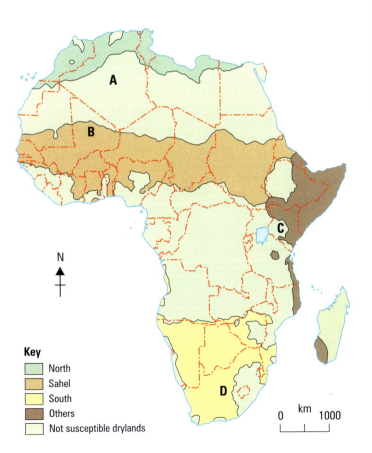

**Key**
- North
- Sahel
- South
- Others
- Not susceptible drylands

N

0 km 1000

▲ **E** *Arid regions of Africa susceptible to soil erosion*

# Damming the Narmada River

India gets 28 per cent of its electricity from hydro-electric power, but as its economy grows, more electricity is needed. The Indian government favours big projects such as the Narmada project. This involves building two superdams, one at Sardar Sarovar, the other at Narmada Sagar. There will also be 30 large dams, 130 medium ones and 3000 minor ones along the Narmada and its **tributaries**.

## The aims of the Narmada project

The Indian government expects the project to:
● provide water for irrigation in Gujarat, an arid part of India with a population of 20 million
● provide water, and generate 1450 megawatts of cheap electricity to boost industrial development across Gujarat state
● provide protection from flooding for 750 000 people.

| West Gujarat | Jan | Feb | Mar | Apr | May | Jun | Jul | Aug | Sep | Oct | Nov | Dec |
|---|---|---|---|---|---|---|---|---|---|---|---|---|
| Temp (°C) | 19 | 20 | 24 | 27.5 | 30 | 31 | 30 | 29.5 | 28 | 27.5 | 24 | 20 |
| Rainfall (mm) | 13 | 10 | 7 | 3 | 3 | 18 | 81 | 40 | 13 | 3 | 3 | 7 |

| Nagpur | Jan | Feb | Mar | Apr | May | Jun | Jul | Aug | Sep | Oct | Nov | Dec |
|---|---|---|---|---|---|---|---|---|---|---|---|---|
| Temp (°C) | 21 | 24 | 28.5 | 32.5 | 35 | 32 | 27.5 | 27 | 27.5 | 26 | 22.5 | 20 |
| Rainfall (mm) | 10 | 18 | 15 | 15 | 20 | 224 | 370 | 290 | 203 | 56 | 20 | 13 |

◀ **B** *Climate data*

▶ **C** *Climate in Ahmadabad, Gujarat*

▼ **A** *The Narmada River basin*

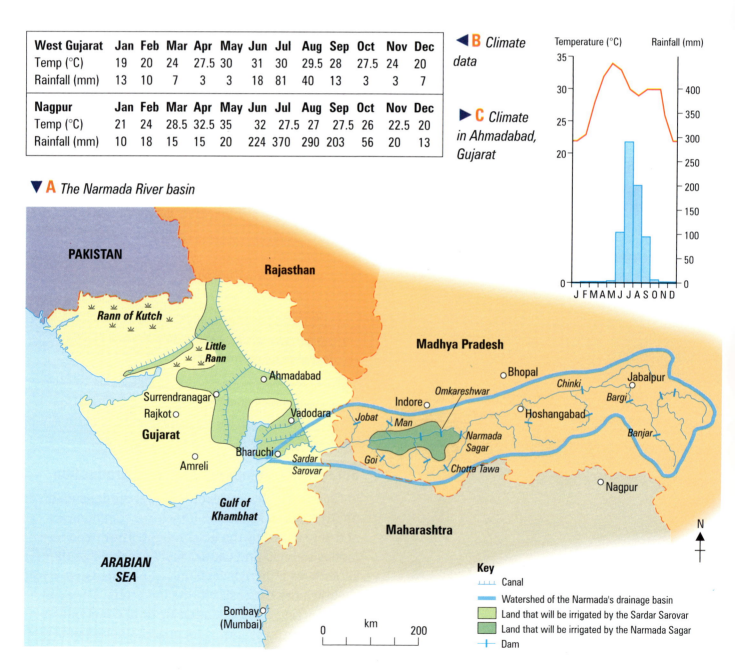

Key
Canal
Watershed of the Narmada's drainage basin
Land that will be irrigated by the Sardar Sarovar
Land that will be irrigated by the Narmada Sagar
Dam

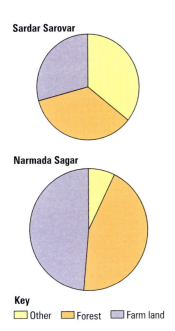

**Sardar Sarovar**

**Narmada Sagar**

**Key**
Other  Forest  Farm land

▲ **D** *The area submerged by the two superdams*

◀ **E** *The Sardar Sarovar Dam at 60m. When complete it will be 120m tall*

## What are the issues in Gujarat?

The aim of the Sardar Sarovar reservoir is to solve the water problem in the dry state of Gujarat. Canals will carry water from the reservoir to areas of drought. However, it is feared that much of the water will go to the rich cotton-growing areas and not to the small rural communities that need it. The huge cost of aqueducts needed to transport the water may outweigh the benefits, especially since existing canals leak badly.

## What are the issues in Madhya Pradesh?

Up to 1.5 million people will lose their homes and have to be settled elsewhere. Local people fear that they will not be properly compensated. The Narmada Sagar reservoir will submerge 90 000 hectares of land, and will only irrigate 123 000 hectares. Deforestation and the increased grazing of livestock in the area will lead to soil erosion. Not only will the farm land suffer, but soil erosion will lead to silting-up of the reservoirs.

---

**1** Use map A. Copy and complete the following. The Narmada flows from ....... to ....... . It is .......km from its source to its mouth in the Gulf of ....... .

**2 a)** In which state is:
   (i) the Sardar Sarovar Dam
   (ii) the largest part of the Narmada drainage basin?
   **b)** Which state has no major dams on the Narmada?

**3** Which of the two superdams will submerge
   **a)** mainly farm land?
   **b)** 35 per cent forest?

**4 a)** Use the data in table B to draw a climate graph for West Gujarat and Nagpur.
   **b)** Use your graphs and climate graph C to describe how the climate changes as you travel from the source of the Narmada westwards to Gujarat's border with Pakistan.
   **c)** Use these graphs to help explain the aim of the Sardar Sarovar Dam.

**5** *Summarize the main advantages and disadvantages of the Narmada project using these headings:*

   ***Impact on people      Impact on the environment***

# The Narmada project debate

▲ **A** *The Narmada project is extremely controversial*

▼ **B** *Changes in India's agricultural and industrial output*

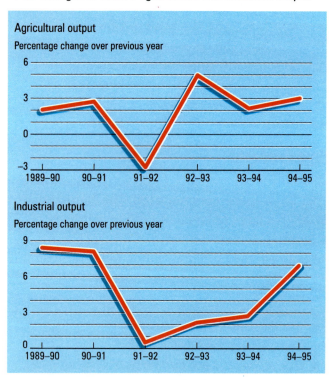

1 Using graph B, describe how India's economy is growing.

2 a) Working in groups of four, produce line graphs to show India's growing electricity production.

   b) Describe the trend of each graph you have drawn. Which is growing faster, and which slower?

   c) Why does the Indian government believe that the Narmada project is necessary?

## The economic argument

India relies heavily on hydro-electric power, as you can see from table C. There are already fourteen superdams, and many more are planned. But still the state power companies cannot keep up with demand, and power cuts are common. At peak times, 20 per cent more electricity is needed than is being produced. Meanwhile, the Indian economy is growing quickly. Exports rose by 20 per cent in 1994. Government ministers believe that the benefits of large-scale projects will 'trickle down' to help the poor.

▼ **C** *India's annual electricity output 1950–1993 (billions kilowatt-hours)*

| Year | HEP | Thermal | Nuclear | Non-utility* | Total |
|------|-----|---------|---------|--------------|-------|
| 1950–51 | 2.5 | 2.6 | - | 1.5 | 6.6 |
| 1960–61 | 7.8 | 9.1 | - | 3.2 | 20.1 |
| 1970–71 | 25.2 | 28.2 | 2.4 | 5.4 | 61.2 |
| 1980–81 | 46.5 | 61.3 | 3.0 | 8.4 | 119.2 |
| 1990–91 | 71.7 | 186.8 | 6.1 | 24.1 | 288.7 |
| 1991–92 | 72.5 | 208.6 | 5.6 | 27.5 | 314.2 |
| 1992–93 | 69.8 | 224.4 | 6.7 | 30.0 | 330.9 |

\* mainly biogas projects

## The rights of tribal peoples

The Narmada project will flood a total area of $3500km^2$ of forest and $600km^2$ of productive farm land. Up to 1.5 million people will lose their homes and have to be settled elsewhere. The majority of the people to be resettled are tribal communities such as Bhils, Pardhans, and Kols who have created a subsistence way of life based on farming, fishing, and forestry. Families who have to move have been promised five hectares of land each, but most will be offered poor quality grazing land in exchange for their once rich land close to the river. Over-grazing and deforestation of this drier land will lead to soil erosion.

Some tribals have already been relocated and are now working in cotton factories. For the first time they are earning money, but they have lost their communities, their traditional way of life, and their culture. There is a strong anti-dam feeling among the tribals who cannot see any benefits for themselves. Some feel so strongly that they say they would rather drown in their homes than move.

## Environmental impacts of the irrigation scheme

The Sardar Sarovar Dam will provide irrigation water for Gujarat. Environmentalists fear that irrigating this arid region will cause the water table to rise. The soil will become waterlogged and natural species of plants will die. **Salination** will also be a problem, as shown in diagram D. All water contains some dissolved salts from the rocks it has passed over or through. Irrigation causes the concentrations of these salts to increase, eventually making the soil useless for farming.

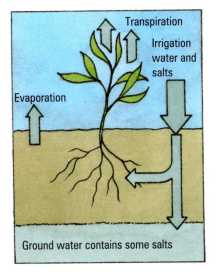

Transpiration

Irrigation water and salts

Evaporation

Ground water contains some salts

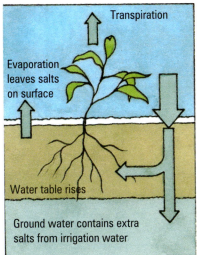

Transpiration

Evaporation leaves salts on surface

Water table rises

Ground water contains extra salts from irrigation water

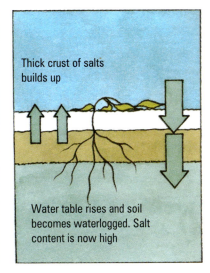

Thick crust of salts builds up

Water table rises and soil becomes waterlogged. Salt content is now high

◀ **D** *Irrigation and leaking canals can lead to salination*

## Dams and asses

The Wildlife Institute of India's four year study reveals that the canals will disrupt the Little Rann of Kutch (LRK) salt flat ecosystem, much of which is now a wild ass sanctuary. The plan is to build a 438km main canal and 35 branch canals totalling 2600km. Eight of the canals will pass close to and possibly through the LRK, isolating the animals within it, bringing high levels of soil moisture and killing 'the plant species which are drought tolerant and salt tolerant.' The changes will also affect other species, including blackbuck, desert fox, and spiny-tailed lizard.

**E** *Extract from* BBC Wildlife, *March 1995*

**3 a)** Using diagram D, explain why irrigation causes:
   (i) the water table to rise
   (ii) salts to become concentrated in the soil.
**b)** Why could installing land drains reduce the problem of salination?

**4 a)** Imagine that you have to tell people that their homes will be flooded and they will have to move elsewhere. Discuss how you would do it. Remember, you must try to persuade them that it is for the best.
**b)** Discuss how you would go about protesting against the scheme. Design a leaflet or speech to inform people of your plight.

## Review

Superdams are being built in many developing countries. The main aims are:
● to generate power
● to provide water for agriculture and industry
● to control flooding.
However, smaller scale schemes are not as costly and do not involve large-scale resettlement or loss of land. They provide a more sustainable form of development.

**5** Design a poster or leaflet describing the advantages and disadvantages of superdams.

**6** Review this unit by describing the aims of the Akosombo, Three Gorges, and Narmada projects.

# 7 Ecotourism

The worldwide tourist industry employs 204 million people.
As tourism grows it has an effect on the natural environment.

- Can tourism continue to grow and the environment be protected at the same time?
- Does ecotourism offer a sustainable form of development in the tourist industry?

## Global tourism

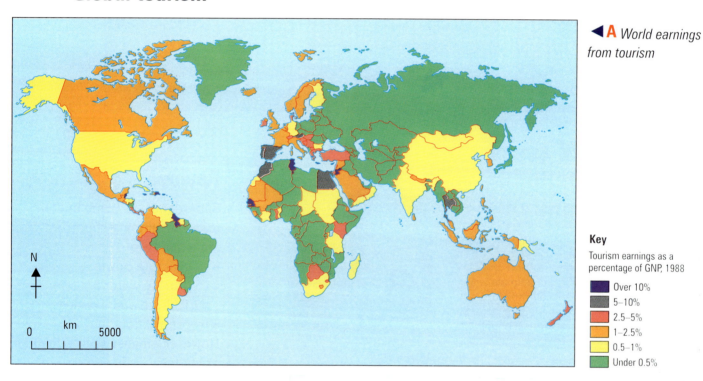

◀ **A** *World earnings from tourism*

**Key**
Tourism earnings as a percentage of GNP, 1988

- Over 10%
- 5–10%
- 2.5–5%
- 1–2.5%
- 0.5–1%
- Under 0.5%

The tourist industry is the world's biggest employer. Across the world tourists spend more than US $1000 million every day. Cheap air flights and package holidays allow millions of people to travel all over the world. As tourists travel to more distant and exotic places, they have an impact on fragile environments such as **rainforests**, savanna, and **coral reefs**. While **tourism** is estimated to generate one in nine of all jobs in the world, do local people always benefit from tourism?

1 Use map A and an atlas to name one country in each of the following regions that earns more than 5 per cent of its GNP from tourism:
   a) Central America   b) West Africa
   c) North Africa   d) South-east Asia
   e) southern Europe.

2 What percentage of their income does each of the following countries earn from tourism:
   a) Turkey   b) Kenya   c) India
   d) Sri Lanka   e) Brazil?

# GOA

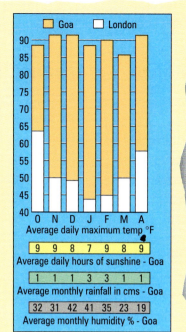

Goa has superb white beaches and gently swaying palms and is ideal for a relaxing holiday. The land is full of scenic charm and abounds with historic forts, magnificent churches, mosques and temples perched among the rice paddy fields. Yoked oxen take shade under the great banyan trees. Indian people are courteous and welcoming, making you feel an honoured guest in their country, where you will experience a culture shock and a slower pace of life.

▲ **B** *Extract from Thomson's* Worldwide *brochure*

Average daily maximum temp °F

| | | | | | | |
|---|---|---|---|---|---|---|
| 9 | 9 | 8 | 7 | 9 | 8 | 9 |

Average daily hours of sunshine - Goa

| | | | | | | |
|---|---|---|---|---|---|---|
| 1 | 1 | 1 | 3 | 3 | 1 | 1 |

Average monthly rainfall in cms - Goa

| | | | | | | |
|---|---|---|---|---|---|---|
| 32 | 31 | 42 | 41 | 35 | 23 | 19 |

Average monthly humidity % - Goa

## Too many tourists?

Countries are keen to attract tourists because they provide work for the local people and bring in money. But as tourist numbers multiply, the needs of local people and the environment are often ignored. Without careful planning, small picturesque resorts become overgrown and ugly, destroying the attraction the tourists came to see. One area under threat is Goa, in India. In Goa, problems have occurred because of the rapid growth of **mass tourism**. Large tourist resorts in India are having a harmful effect on the environment. Tourist numbers in Goa have risen from 10 000 in 1972 to over a million in 1995. In 1994 2.4 million tourists visited India.

▶ **C** *From* The Independent on Sunday, *12 February 1995*

# Mass tourism is poisoning a paradise

With a rich mixture of Portuguese and Indian culture, and 105km of coastline – two-thirds of it sandy beaches fringed with coconut palms – Goa is expecting five million tourists by the end of the century. But Tourism Concern says Goa's 'fragile ecology and unique culture are being systematically destroyed by hotel owners eager to cash in on the growing influx of tourists'. Hotels have been sited illegally on the beach, beaches have been closed to locals, threatened mangrove and wetlands areas have been reclaimed in breach of the law, sand has been quarried from beaches, trees felled and dunes levelled to make artificial lawns. Sewage is being discharged onto beaches or leaking into paddy fields.

**3 a)** Use resource B to suggest three reasons why tourists might want to visit Goa.
**b)** Compare the winter climate of Goa with that of London.

**4 a)** Explain the term mass tourism.
**b)** Why is Goa a good example of mass tourism?
**c)** How important is Goa to India's tourist industry?

**5** Consider the impact of tourism on Goa, and complete a table like the one below:

| | Advantages of tourism | Disadvantages of tourism |
|---|---|---|
| For local people | | |
| For the environment | | |

# Belize: tourism and the natural environment

Belize is a small tropical country in Central America. In the past it relied on the export of crops such as coconuts, but the value of these exports is falling. Tourism is now the country's second highest earner and the fastest growing sector of the economy. Belize has plenty to offer the tourist – a tropical climate, sandy beaches, Mayan archaeology, and the second largest barrier reef in the world. But in contrast to Goa, Belize aims to develop small-scale tourist projects that will help protect the environment – a concept known as **ecotourism**.

## Mangrove: wasteland or wetland habitat?

**Mangrove** trees grow near the coast where fresh river water is mixed with sea water by the tide. Mangroves are usually regarded as useless wastelands. All around the world mangroves are being cut down and the swampy land drained ready for development – often to build a tourist resort.

▲ **A** *Mangrove destruction*

Mangrove is a rich ecosystem, supporting a range of animals including howler monkeys, deer, armadillo, crocodile, snakes, and crabs

Mangroves act as natural coastal defence, protecting the land from erosion

Mangrove timber can be a valuable resource

Large prop roots support the tree above high tide. They trap fine sediment carried in the water, causing it to be deposited

Mangroves provide breeding grounds for fish, and nesting sites for birds

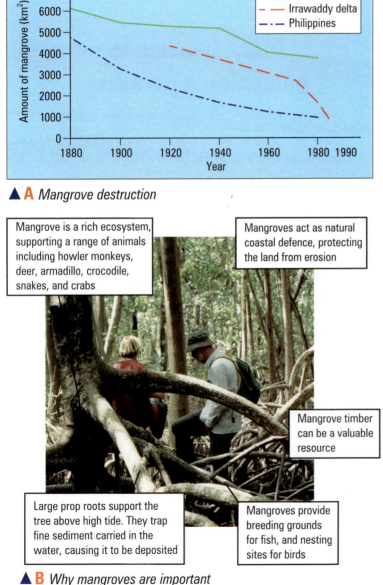

▲ **B** *Why mangroves are important*

▼ **C** *Belize in Central America*

**Key**

■ Forest reserves     ■ Bird reserves     — Roads
□ Coral reef     □ Other wildlife reserves

# High tech solutions to environmental protection

Only by knowing where certain habitats are located can the planners prevent delicate wildlife habitats from being destroyed. For 20 years, a team of geographers from the University of Edinburgh has been helping the Belizean government to map the country's vegetation. Diagram D shows how it is done. This information helps plan the growth of tourism and protect the environment. The government has established nature reserves, wildlife parks, and conservation areas. Sixteen forest reserves have been established, covering around 7000km$^2$.

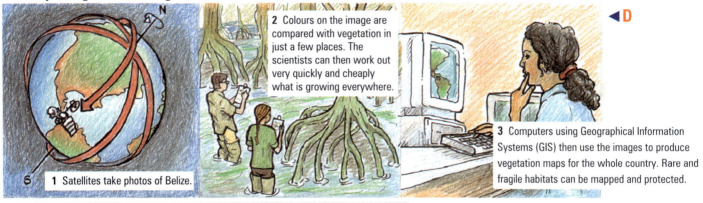

**1** Satellites take photos of Belize.

**2** Colours on the image are compared with vegetation in just a few places. The scientists can then work out very quickly and cheaply what is growing everywhere.

**3** Computers using Geographical Information Systems (GIS) then use the images to produce vegetation maps for the whole country. Rare and fragile habitats can be mapped and protected.

◀ **D**

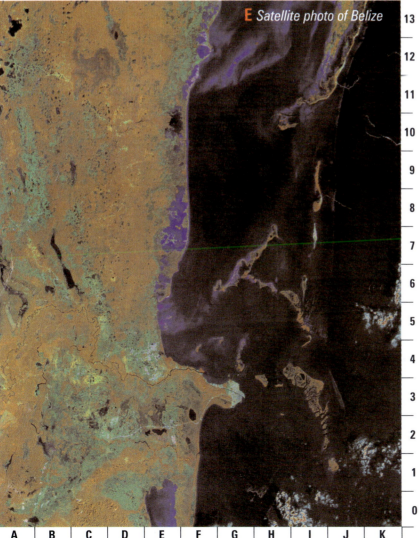

**E** *Satellite photo of Belize*

**1** Use map C. How long is the Belize coastline?

**2** Use graph A.
   **a)** How much mangrove was there in the Irrawaddy delta in 1920 and in 1980?
   **b)** What percentage of mangrove has been lost in the Irrawaddy delta?
   (i) 25 per cent (ii) 50 per cent (iii) 75 per cent?
   **c)** Which country is losing mangrove at the fastest rate?

**3** Write a letter to the Philippine government explaining why mangroves are important and persuading them to protect what remains of their mangrove swamps.

**4** What are the advantages of GIS for mapping a country?

**5** Refer to map C and satellite image E.
   **a)** Give grid references for:
   (i) Belize City   (ii) Ambergris Cay.
   **b)** What colours on the satellite image show:
   (i) shallow water   (ii) forests?

▲ A *Mayan temple – a potential tourist site?*

## The needs of local people

The population of Belize includes 9 per cent of people descended from the Mayan Indians who built beautiful pyramids like the one in photo A. Most Mayans are farmers who clear small patches of rainforest to grow maize and vegetables for their own use, and fruit to sell. Slash and burn farming, as this is called, and logging, have formed a patchwork of rainforest at different stages of growth and regrowth. If farmers cut down more forest, and Belize were deforested, the habitat of animals like the black howler monkey would be lost forever. How can the Mayans have a higher standard of living whilst preserving the rainforest and their Mayan culture? One answer may be ecotourism.

## The Bermudian Landing ecotourism project

At Bermudian Landing the rainforest habitat of the howler monkey was threatened by slash and burn clearance for agriculture. The local community decided to try an experiment in ecotourism. Farmers were encouraged to leave thick hedgerows of rainforest trees around their fields. The population of black howler monkeys has increased by 30 per cent in the first five years of the reserve. Around 3000 tourists visit this baboon sanctuary every year. The local community are not allowed to charge an entrance fee, but they do encourage tourists to stay in their homes for a small fee. There is no hotel and no mains water. Tourists bathe in the river or in water drawn from the well.

## Belize – the lucky country

An essential factor in ecotourism is the preservation and protection of Belize's natural assets: her reef, cays, rainforest, rivers, streams, Mayan ruins, wild lands, and wildlife. On occasion, a few acres of eel grass or stands of mangrove must be sacrificed; otherwise development, and the jobs that it will bring in agriculture and tourism, will be stifled.

▲ B *Extract from* The Belize Review, *June 1990*

▼ C *A black howler monkey, known as a baboon to the Mayans*

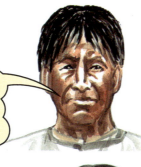

**▼ E** *Mayan opinions on tourism*

> Tourists enjoy staying out here and get an experience of our culture and our style of living.

> We had a problem with visitors bringing packed lunches with them. They wanted to leave their wrappers and cans but we have no way of getting rid of the garbage. Now the visitors eat lunch with families in the village.

**▲ D** *A Mayan Indian village*

# Tourism by invitation only!

The Quichua people of Capirona, in Ecuador, are doing something rather strange. In order to protect their traditional way of life and 2000 hectares of rainforest, they are promoting tourism. The package they are offering is geared to their needs, not the whims of tourists. The aim is to teach visitors in detail about the immense value of the rainforest to the community and to the wider world. You won't find details in your local travel agent's window. Rather, the community is contacting colleges and environmental groups who have a serious interest in the preservation of primary rainforest. The head of the community outlines five aims: to protect the forest; to keep the community together; to build a good new school for the children; to provide a health centre; and slowly, but surely, to improve the standard of living.

**► F** *Extract from Common Cause, January 1993*

**1** Explain what is meant by the term **ecotourism**.

**2 a)** How many visitors come to Bermudian Landing every year?

**b)** What two things would have to be done to increase this number? Refer to map C on page 74.

**c)** Do you think it would be good to increase the number of visitors? Explain your answer.

**3 a)** In what ways do the local communities benefit from the ecotourism project at the Bermudian Landing Baboon Sanctuary?

**b)** How has the environment benefited?

**c)** What environmental problem did the project come across, and how was this problem solved?

**4** Read extract F.

**a)** What might the Mayans learn from this project to develop their own ecotourism?

**b)** *One of the Indians in Ecuador says, 'Regular tourism exists in the province, but it tends to be boat trips where **indigenous** communities are pointed out like objects on the river bank.' What impact might tourism have on the Mayan people? Consider both good and bad effects.*

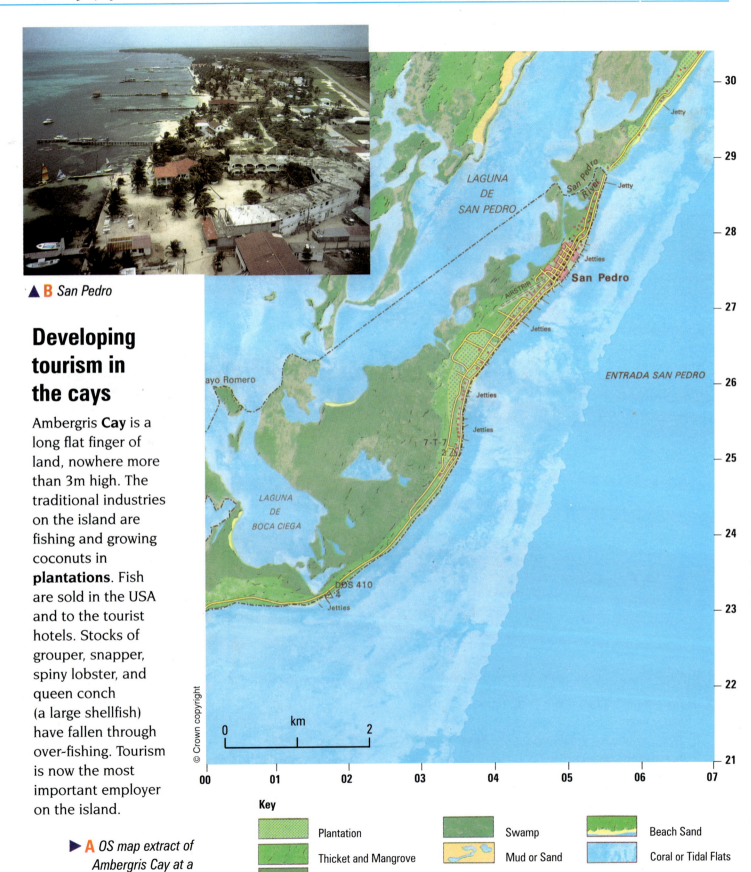

▲ **B** *San Pedro*

# Developing tourism in the cays

Ambergris **Cay** is a long flat finger of land, nowhere more than 3m high. The traditional industries on the island are fishing and growing coconuts in **plantations**. Fish are sold in the USA and to the tourist hotels. Stocks of grouper, snapper, spiny lobster, and queen conch (a large shellfish) have fallen through over-fishing. Tourism is now the most important employer on the island.

▶ **A** *OS map extract of Ambergris Cay at a scale of 1:50 000*

LAGUNA DE SAN PEDRO

San Pedro River

Jetty

Jetty

Jetty

San Pedro

Jetties

AIRSTRIP

Jetties

ENTRADA SAN PEDRO

Jetties

Cayo Romero

Jetties

7-T-7
2 △

LAGUNA DE BOCA CIEGA

DOS 410
△ 4

Jetties

© Crown copyright

0    km    2

**Key**

| | | |
|---|---|---|
| Plantation | Swamp | Beach Sand |
| Thicket and Mangrove | Mud or Sand | Coral or Tidal Flats |
| Mangrove | | |

Hol Chan marine reserve, 6km south-south-west of San Pedro, was established in 1987. The reserve is divided into zones where fishing and diving are restricted. Tourists pay an admission charge. An information pack explains the rules of the reserve and shows where they are allowed to go. Marine scientists continually monitor the reef and fish stocks, and compare the information with areas outside the reserve.

Any environment can suffer if too many people visit it. Footpaths in the UK's national parks are widened because too many walkers trample them. The number of people an environment can withstand before it is damaged is known as its **carrying capacity**. A fragile environment has a smaller carrying capacity than a rugged one. Coral is very fragile; just touching it can kill it. A lot of damage is done by anchors from tourist and fishing boats. Algae is another problem. Algae grows on damaged coral, and thrives on untreated sewage discharged into the sea from the tourist hotel areas.

DEAD CORAL

LIVING CORAL

▲ **C** *Coral*

Up to 250 people visit the reserve every day. Some stand on the reef or break off pieces of coral. Black band coral disease attacks the coral, especially in tourist areas. The reef is suffering increased environmental stress.

One solution is to ban tourists from certain areas altogether. Another is to create lots of reserves so that the tourist damage in any one place is reduced. By encouraging tourists to visit specific areas, other areas can be spared the damage.

**1** Use map extract A.
  **a)** Describe the shape and size of San Pedro.
  **b)** How far off shore is the edge of the coral reef?
  **c)** Give a grid reference for the Hol Chan marine reserve.
  **d)** In what direction was the camera pointing to take photo B?

**2** List all the ways that tourism can damage the reef.

**3** Suggest reasons why:
  **a)** scientists are monitoring stocks of fish and the condition of the coral
  **b)** fishing and diving are restricted in some areas of the reserve.

**4 a)** Explain what is meant by carrying capacity.
  **b)** Explain the advantages and disadvantages of
    (i) banning tourists from certain areas of the reef
    (ii) spreading them around several reserves.
  **c)** Devise a plan that will allow for tourist development without further damage to the reef. Include:
    (i)  a description of Ambergris Cay, where it is and what it is like;
    (ii) a description of how you think tourism could be developed;
    (iii) a map or diagram showing how your plan would work.

# Developing the desert: tourism in Wadi Rum, Jordan

Jordan is a desert country in the Middle East. Its desert climate and scenery are only part of its attraction. It also has coral reefs in the Red Sea, and many ancient archaeological and historic sites. It is easy to reach for European holiday makers, with a short flight time. Wadi Rum is a small village in the desert. Most tourists visit Wadi Rum on a day trip from Petra or Aqaba by luxury coach. The village is often swamped by hundreds of tourists and big coaches.

JORDAN

▼ **A** *Tourism's impact on Wadi Rum*

- Disposal of sewage and litter is difficult
- Employment and money for local people
- Jeeps erode tracks in the desert surface
- People of different cultures meet and swap ideas

The local people are Bedouin, nomads who keep herds of goats and camels

↓

Tourism creates job opportunities

↓

Bedouin become more settled in the town

↓

Goat herds are no longer taken to graze in other districts

↓

Vegetation around the town is overgrazed

↓

Soil is exposed to the sun and rain

↓

?

▲ **C** *Impact of tourism on the Bedouin people*

▼ **B** *Results of questions asked of tourists in Wadi Rum, Jordan*

| Why did you come to Jordan for a holiday? | % | How long will you stay in Wadi Rum? | No. of people |
|---|---|---|---|
| The desert scenery | 37 | Two hours | 36 |
| The weather | 11 | Six hours | 77 |
| Historical sites | 34 | One day | 45 |
| Biblical sites | 8 | Two days | 29 |
| Other | 10 | Longer | 14 |

**1 a)** Draw suitable graphs to display the information in B.
 **b)** What are Jordan's two main attractions?
 **c)** Suggest why it might benefit local people if the tourists stayed longer.

**2 a)** Use A and C to list the advantages and disadvantages that tourism has brought to Wadi Rum.
 **b)** Study C. Write your own label for the final box.
 **c)** How has tourism altered the customs and culture of the Bedouin people?

## Sustainable tourism in Wadi Rum?

The Jordanian Ministry of Tourism has suggested two plans for Wadi Rum. One plan is to encourage more visitors. Tourists will be persuaded to stay longer at Wadi Rum and spend more money.
To make sure that this causes little damage to the environment, the plan would include:

- creating walking routes through the desert, with overnight camp sites for tourists
- building a visitor centre with information about the desert environment and Wadi Rum
- encouraging the Bedouin to stay in the desert with their herds.

Other specific recommendations for tourist growth are shown on map D.
  The alternative plan is to prevent any further tourist growth. Damage from tourism could be controlled by providing better facilities such as:

- more litter bins
- regular litter collections
- building a road to keep jeeps off the desert.

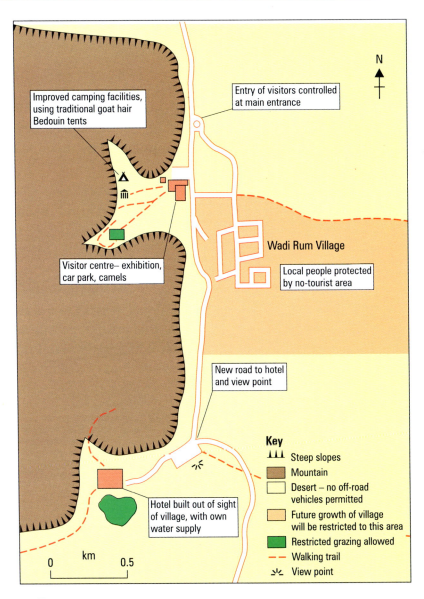

▲ **D** *Sustainable tourist growth*

**3** Imagine that you are a tourist to Wadi Rum. What tourist facilities would you like to see provided or developed?

**4** Consider the two management plans in D and E for Wadi Rum. Which do you think will be best:
  **a)** for the environment
  **b)** for local people?

**5** Suggest your own management plan for developing ecotourism in Wadi Rum. Include a map of the town, and sketches or diagrams of any features you might construct, such as accommodation.

## Review

In this unit we have learned that:

- the tourist industry is growing and provides valuable income for many countries
- the cost and benefits of tourism must be balanced
- the environment is a valuable resource for tourism
- ecotourism and sustainable development allow for tourism to grow with a minimum of damage to the environment.

# 8 Brazil

In this unit we will examine the development issues facing Brazil.
- **What is Brazil like? Are all its regions the same?**
- **Why is 50 per cent of its population living in poverty when it is so rich in resources?**
- **How can Brazil create a fairer society?**
- **How can Brazil continue to use its natural resources, without damaging the environment?**

BRAZIL

## A giant country

Brazil is huge. Covering 8.5 million km² (nearly half of South America), it is bigger than the European Union. It has the eighth largest economy in the world, and exports more iron ore, coffee, sugar cane, and oranges than any other country in the world. But despite Brazil's economic and industrial successes, many Brazilians live in poverty.

Brazil contains most of the huge Amazonian rainforest. The river Amazon running through it contains more water than any other river on Earth

Brazil contains enormous mineral wealth e.g. 50% of the world's platinum. The world's largest iron ore field is in Carajas, Amazonia

The coastline of mainly unspoilt sandy beaches is the longest in South America (7400km)

73% of Brazilians live in urban areas; the largest cities are in the south-east. São Paulo (15.2m) and Rio de Janeiro (9.6m) are two of the worlds largest cities

**Key**
- Over 1000m
- 500m
- 200m
- 0

km
0        1000

◀ **A**

*Physical features of Brazil*

1 Use map A.
  a) Copy and complete the following: Brazil shares a border with ...... other countries in ...... America. It has a ...... km long coastline on the ...... Ocean. Its largest cities are in the ......-...... region.
  b) Measure Brazil from east to west and from north to south. Look at the lines of latitude and longitude. How big is Brazil compared with other places? Write a sentence about Brazil's size.
  c) Use an atlas to do the same as in **b)** for Europe or Australia.

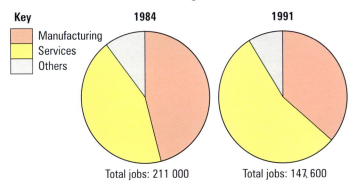

▼ **C** *How work in Stoke has changed*

**Key**
- Manufacturing
- Services
- Others

1984

1991

Total jobs: 211 000

Total jobs: 147 600

## Modern factories

The Potteries are in a very **accessible** area: it is on the M6 and is well connected to the rest of the country. New factories have been attracted to specially designed industrial estates on the outskirts of the city. The large building in photo D is the most automated brick factory in Europe. Most jobs in the brickworks are for highly skilled engineers and technicians who operate the equipment, including a computer-controlled electric kiln.

**1** Using this page to start you off, make a list of ten different jobs. Divide them into jobs that:
   **a)** make something (manufacturing)
   **b)** provide a service.

**2** Using C, what percentage of people were employed in manufacturing in
   **a)** 1984?   **b)** 1991?
   **c)** What new jobs are being created? Use the information on this page to describe how jobs in Stoke have changed.

**3** Describe the site of the factories in photo D. Use words from the following list to help you:
   crowded/plenty of space   flat/hilly land
   good/bad roads   small/large buildings.

**4** In what way are the skills needed by the pottery workers in photo B different from those needed by the workers in the brick factory?

**5** Use map A to describe the location of the new industrial estate in D. Discuss why the new factories are located here. Explain the advantages of being accessible.

▶ **D**  *Parkhouse Industrial Estate in the 1980s*

# Industrial change in the heart of the city

What happens when an industry closes down? How are people and the environment affected? The district of Etruria was at the heart of the old industrial city of Stoke-on-Trent. The canal, railway, potteries, gas works, and steel works were all located here. Study resources A, B, and C to give you an idea of what this area used to be like.

► **A** *Industrial Etruria in the 1930s, by local artist C W Brown*

▼ **B** *Extract from* From Inferno to Flowers *by Elaine Bryan and Neville Fisher, 1986*

When the white hot slag was tipped from the top of the slagheaps, to go cascading down the slope, the glow was reflected on the low cloud of the night sky, and lit the area for miles around. A vivid red at first, then slowly fading in shade and intensity to a dull lingering glow, it alarmed strangers but somehow reassured local folk. Returning travellers knew that they were nearly home when they saw the sky turn red.

▼ **C** *This land use map at 1:25 000 shows what Etruria was like in the 1960s*

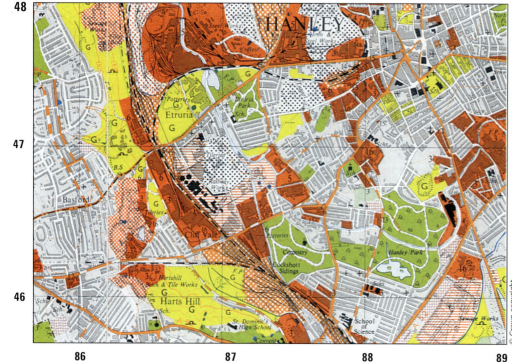

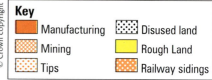

**Key**

| | |
|---|---|
| ▮ Manufacturing | ▦ Disused land |
| ▨ Mining | ▮ Rough Land |
| ▦ Tips | ▨ Railway sidings |

© Crown copyright

**1 a)** Measure the length of the steel works site from map C.

**b)** List the land uses on the map that would have polluted or spoilt the look of the area.

**2 a)** Describe the scene in A using some of the following words: dirty, noisy, bright, lively, dangerous, pollution, busy, crowded.

**b)** Extract B suggests that locals felt differently about the industry than visitors. Why do you think this was, and how do you think that the artist who painted A felt about the area?

**3** Using extracts A, B, and C, try to write about old Etruria's good and bad points.

# Etruria today

The British Steel plant in Etruria closed in 1979. Some 3000 jobs were lost at the site, and others followed in local shops and businesses. The 66 hectare site became a derelict eyesore just 1km from the city centre. The City Council reclaimed the derelict land at a cost of £7.5 million. The site was then landscaped and used to host the 1986 Garden Festival. This cost another £17.45 million, but brought many benefits.

- £8.03 million was earned from ticket sales to the festival.
- £12.5 million worth of contracts were made with local companies, e.g. builders.
- £7.2 million was spent by visitors in local shops, hotels, etc.
- A landscaped site was left, with modern services (roads, water, electricity). This has attracted new industry to the area.

Photos D and E show what the area looks like today. A total of 2500 permanent jobs have been created on the site. Some of them are in small **manufacturing** firms, but most are in shops, offices, and leisure facilities like the cinema. Many of these jobs are unskilled, such as stocking shelves in the shops, and others are part-time.

▼ **D** *Leisure development, grid reference 871479*

▼ **E** *Commercial site, grid reference 873477*

**4** Use the grid references to find out what used to be where the buildings in photos D and E are today.

**5** Write about how the area and jobs have changed in the places shown in the two photos.

**6 a)** How much did it cost to reclaim Etruria and run the Garden Festival?

**b)** How much money did it raise for the area in total?

**c)** Write about the advantages and disadvantages of what has happened in Etruria. You should concentrate on how work and the environment have changed.

# Hong Kong: city of contrasts

Hong Kong is situated on the coast of southern China. It has a population of about 6 million. Hong Kong is a world financial centre. It is also a busy manufacturing city that successfully **exports** goods all over the world, as B shows.

## The Central Business District: jobs in finance and banking

Hong Kong has the second largest stock market in Asia after Tokyo. Eighty-one out of the world's top 100 banks have branches in the city. A total of 9.4% of all employment in Hong Kong is in banking. People in the top jobs are responsible for a lot of money. They work hard, on average 60 hours a week. They are extremely well paid and have their rent and their children's education paid for by their companies. There are also wealthy business people living in the city who own small factories or shops.

## Less well-paid work

Not everyone in Hong Kong is rich. There are many domestic helpers, factory workers, and street hawkers. Over 120000 domestic helpers like Delia in C work in Hong Kong. That's almost equal to all the people working in Stoke-on-Trent put together. As many as 87% of the domestic helpers are from the Philippines.

▼ **B** *Hong Kong's trading partners*

| Country | Exports (%) |
|---|---|
| China | 28 |
| USA | 27 |
| Germany | 6 |
| Singapore | 5 |
| UK | 5 |

| Country | Imports (%) |
|---|---|
| China | 38 |
| Japan | 17 |
| Taiwan | 9 |

▼ **C**

▼ **A** *Inside the Hong Kong and Shanghai Bank Head Office*

I work for a banker as a domestic helper and I live with the family. I work about 70 hours a week. I do the cleaning and cooking for the family, but my biggest responsibility is looking after the children, especially the two youngest. I have children of my own in Manila, Philippines. I've lived apart from them for six years now. I really miss them and I would like to go home, but jobs there are so badly paid. I earn as much here as a doctor would get paid in the Philippines.

## Street hawkers

**Unemployment** in Hong Kong is less than 2%. People who cannot find regular work do all kinds of part-time or casual jobs. Street hawkers selling fruit, vegetables, T-shirts, or watches are a common sight. Other people deliver goods or collect up materials for recycling, like the man in photo D.

Often these people are not paid a regular wage, and they do not pay taxes. The work they do is called '**informal**' and they are breaking local rules. Market traders should pay the local authorities for a licence. There are 12 200 licensed hawkers and an estimated 6400 unlicensed hawkers. In 1993 there were 85 000 convictions for illegal hawking.

▼ **D** *Collecting cardboard from the market for recycling*

▼ **E** *Women prepare vegetables for the market*

**1** What similarities and differences are there between the wealthy bankers and business people and the domestic helpers they employ?

**2** What advice would you give to Delia? Should she stay or go? Give reasons for your answer.

**3** Use photos D and E, and the text above.
 **a)** Explain what makes informal work different from other work we have studied.
 **b)** Why do you think unemployment is so low?

 **c)** Why do you think the city authority fines unlicensed hawkers?

**4 a)** Draw a map or graph to show Hong Kong's trading partners. Divided bars, pies, or a world map would all be suitable.
 **b)** Describe the pattern shown by your map or graph. With what parts of the world does Hong Kong mostly trade?

# How are jobs changing in Hong Kong?

Hong Kong has virtually no **raw materials**, it has to **import** all the materials needed for its industries from other countries. Its factories produce mainly light consumer goods like clothing, plastics, and electronics; 80% of these goods are then exported. Hong Kong has the busiest container port in the world, and the third busiest airport. The total value of Hong Kong's exports in 1993 was US$82185 million (the UK had exports worth US$185891 million and a population of 58 million).

▶ **A** *Cargo is still unloaded by hand from the small ships that come from China*

▼ **B** *The main urban areas of Hong Kong*

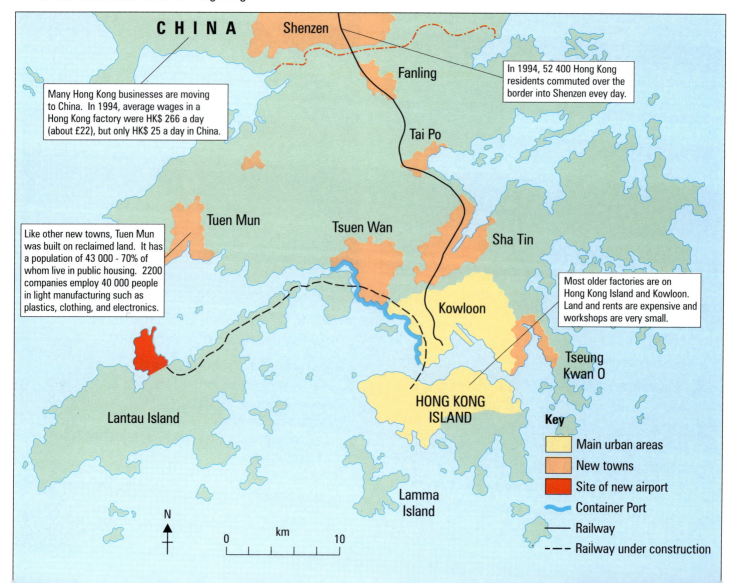

Many Hong Kong businesses are moving to China. In 1994, average wages in a Hong Kong factory were HK$ 266 a day (about £22), but only HK$ 25 a day in China.

In 1994, 52 400 Hong Kong residents commuted over the border into Shenzen evey day.

Like other new towns, Tuen Mun was built on reclaimed land. It has a population of 43 000 - 70% of whom live in public housing. 2200 companies employ 40 000 people in light manufacturing such as plastics, clothing, and electronics.

Most older factories are on Hong Kong Island and Kowloon. Land and rents are expensive and workshops are very small.

**CHINA** · Shenzen · Fanling · Tai Po · Tuen Mun · Tsuen Wan · Sha Tin · Kowloon · Tseung Kwan O · Lantau Island · HONG KONG ISLAND · Lamma Island

N

0   km   10

**Key**
- Main urban areas
- New towns
- Site of new airport
- Container Port
- Railway
- Railway under construction

## Manufacturing

If you walk through the back streets of Hong Kong, you will see hundreds of small workshops. Small businesses make T-shirts, repair electrical goods, print, or make metal parts for air-conditioners, like the man in photo C. Next door might be a shop or street market. Many families live in the tower block above. This may seem noisy and dangerous but workers do not have far to travel to work. Hong Kong's government encourages these small firms. Over 88% of manufacturing firms employ less than twenty people. Many of these are in the urban areas on Hong Kong Island and Kowloon.

## Industrial change in Hong Kong

In the last five years the number of jobs in manufacturing has declined. Some companies have moved to China where the workers are paid less. For example, the loss of jobs in the clothing industry can be seen in graph D. It was Hong Kong's biggest employer. Other companies have introduced new technology, as you can see in photo E. Between 1984 and 1993 the percentage of people employed in manufacturing fell from 42% to 21%.

1 How many people were employed in the clothing industry in 1983 and 1993?

2 Between 1984 and 1993 the percentage of people employed in manufacturing fell from 42% to 21%. Use these data to produce two pie charts.

3 In what ways are the factories in Hong Kong similar to or different from the ones in Stoke? Make notes using the following headings: products, size of firm, location of the factories, skills.

4 a) Describe how employment in Hong Kong is changing.
  b) Look back at C on page 39 and the information on pages 40–41. Describe the similarities between changes in employment in Hong Kong and Stoke-on-Trent.

5 *Compare the value of Hong Kong's exports with the exports from the UK. Remember to take the size of the population into account.*

▼ **D** *The loss of jobs in the clothing industry*
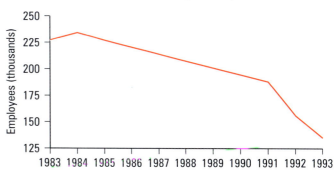

▼ **C** *A metal worker shapes part of an air-conditioning duct outside his small workshop*

▼ **E** *Computer-aided design in the Neil Pryde Sailmaking Company*

# Self-help in the city

Apart from the street hawkers in Hong Kong, most of the workers we have seen in this unit get paid a regular wage. But what happens if you are unemployed or only work part-time in the city? What other kinds of work are available?

## Work in the *favelas* of Rio de Janeiro

Rio de Janeiro in Brazil has a population of 9.6 million. Around 3 million people in Rio live in *favelas* (**shanty towns**). Many people who live in the *favelas* work in the shops and factories of Rio doing regular paid jobs. Others do informal work, like street hawking. People meet regularly to discuss how to improve the *favela*. Work parties spend the weekends improving the footpaths and steps through the settlement. They also help each other improve their homes, or work on a community building like the crèche in photo A.

▲ **A** *Volunteers give up their weekend to build a new crèche in the* favela

1  What evidence is there that people in the *favelas* are well organized and have a strong sense of community?

2  **a)** Use photo A to describe the kinds of building materials used in the *favelas*.

   **b)** What kinds of skills do the volunteer workers in the *favela* need?

Cities in the developing world have been growing very fast. Local governments find it difficult to provide services and homes for the people who move there. Many of these people make their homes in shanty towns. Often they have no electricity, piped water, or sewage system. Despite this, these communities are often the most lively and growing part of a city economy.

As graph B shows, in some cities there are more people living in the shanty towns than in proper houses.

▼ **B** *Percentage of people living in shanty towns in cities in the developing world*

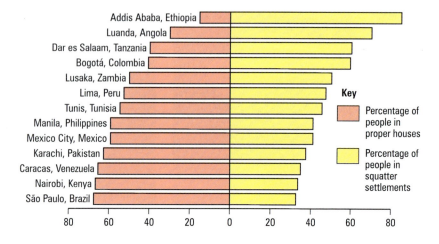

Key

■ Percentage of people in proper houses

■ Percentage of people in squatter settlements

## Self-build projects in the UK

There are now 25 000 people building their own homes in the UK. Many are young unemployed people. They get the chance to build a home that they can then rent cheaply, and learn practical skills like joinery, plumbing, and electrical work at the same time. These skills will hopefully help them find regular work after the house is built.

▲ **C** *Working on a self-help building project*

**3** In what ways do the young people in the self-build projects in the UK benefit?

**4** Do you think the self-build project is a good idea?

### Building a home and a future

One self-build scheme is in Maltby, South Yorkshire, a mining town with high unemployment. Seven men and two women, between the ages of 19 and 30, started building their homes in August; when they have finished, they will be able to rent the homes.

The young self-builders have been given a 10-week training course in brickwork and joinery and while they build they receive £10 a week on top of state benefit. It is hoped that by the time they have finished the project in 18 months' time, they will each pass NVQ Level 2 in their chosen skill.

▲ **D** *Extract adapted from* The Times, *2 November 1994*

## Review

There are all kinds of work available in the city. There are jobs in factories and jobs that provide a service, like shop or hotel work. Most of these workers get paid a regular wage. Other jobs are informal, like street hawking. These jobs are more irregular and workers usually do not pay tax.

Other people work without getting paid at all, like the self-build workers.

**5** Look back through the unit. Make a list of the kinds of work we have studied. Now try to fit the work into categories using the headings below.
- Manufacturing – skilled manual work
- Manufacturing – skilled technicians
- Service industries
- Informal work
- Unpaid work.

**6** Discuss what other kinds of work belong to this last category of unpaid work. Add them to your list.

# 5 Kenya

Kenya is in East Africa. Kenya is changing and in order to understand these changes we need to answer the following questions:

- what is Kenya's environment like?
- why is Kenya attractive to tourists and what impact does tourism have on the environment?
- what is life like for people in rural and urban areas? Why do people move to the city? How can rural life be improved?

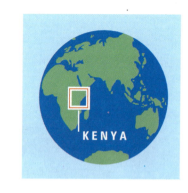

KENYA

▼ A Kenya's natural vegetation

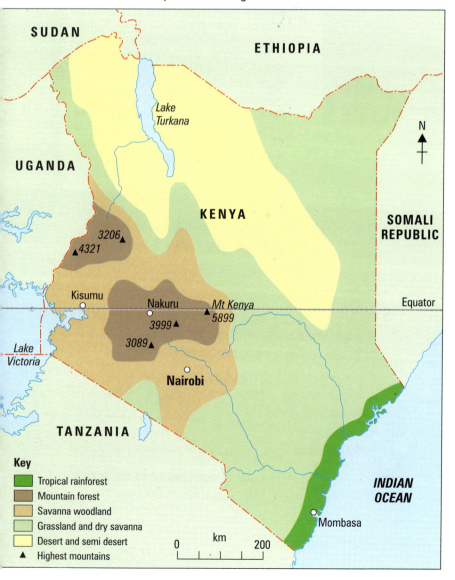

**Key**
- ■ Tropical rainforest
- ■ Mountain forest
- ■ Savanna woodland
- ■ Grassland and dry savanna
- ■ Desert and semi desert
- ▲ Highest mountains

## Kenya's natural environment

Tropical rainforest is found along Kenya's eastern coastline. This region is lush and green, very hot and wet. The rainforest forms a dense barrier to the great variety of scenery beyond. Some of the rainforest has been cleared for agriculture. There are now many small plantations of bananas, pineapples, and coconuts.

### Factfile: Kenya

- Mount Kenya, which is on the Equator, is over 5000 m high. Its peak is snow-capped.
- Kenya has the highest **birth rate** in the world.
- Nearly 50% of its people are under 15.
- It is the fourth biggest tea producer in the world.
- Some of the oldest human bones ever discovered were found in Kenya.

**1** Using map A, measure the approximate length of the tropical rainforest in kilometres.

**2** What area of land (as a percentage) is covered by:
  **a)** grassland and dry savanna?
  **b)** savanna woodland?

# On safari

Beyond the rainforest the interior of Kenya is very dry. The dry grasslands have only sparse bushes with an occasional tree; this landscape is called **savanna**. It is difficult to grow many crops. The northern area around Lake Turkana is desert. It receives less than 250mm of rain each year. The south-west of Kenya receives a lot more rain so the landscape is green, with many trees. More land is cultivated for crops here than anywhere else in Kenya.

Kenya's varied environment and wildlife attract more and more tourists each year. Huge areas of savanna have been made National Reserves or National Parks to protect the wildlife. These cover 8% of Kenya's land. In the Maasai Mara you can observe the wildlife in two ways: by bus, up to nine people at a time, or by an early morning flight in a hot-air balloon.

The safari bus lets you get much closer to the animals. However, the buses disturb the animals and the tyres rip up the vegetation. The air balloons do not destroy the landscape but the burner is very noisy and some of the animals, such as gazelles, are frightened by it.

▲ **C** Tropical rainforest along the Kenyan coast

▶ **D** Tourism earns a large part of Kenya's income

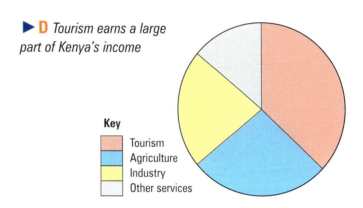

**Key**

- Tourism
- Agriculture
- Industry
- Other services

▼ **B** Morning flight over the savanna landscape of the Maasai Mara

**3** Look at photos B and C. List the differences you can see in the vegetation.

**4** What makes the Parks or Reserves attractive to tourists?

**5 a)** Look at D. What percentage of Kenya's income comes from tourism?

**b)** Describe the possible problems that tourism may cause.

**6** As a visitor to the Maasai Mara, decide how you are going to make your trip across the Reserve. Which method of travel will give you the best views of the animals, let you see more of the countryside, and cause least damage? Draw a table of Advantages/Disadvantages for the safari bus and the hot-air balloon and fill it in.

# Kenya's coastline – a tropical paradise?

▲ **A** *Watamu Beach, Malindi*

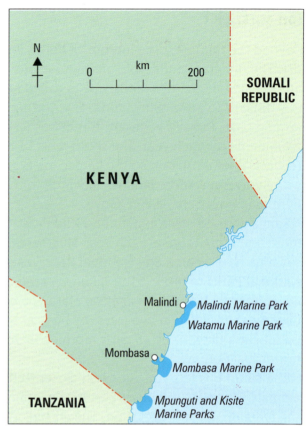

▲ **C** *The coastline of Kenya*

Tourists are attracted to Kenya's beaches as well as to the wildlife of the savanna. Kenya's coastline lies just south of the Equator. There is plenty of sunshine and high temperatures throughout the year, although there is a rainy season from April to May. With this 'Tropical Paradise' **climate** it is not surprising that Kenya's beautiful coastline has become a fast-growing tourist area, particularly for people from Europe, including Britain, and from the USA.

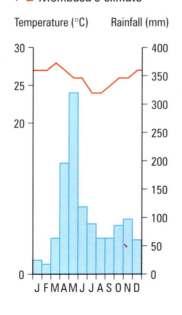

▼ **B** *Mombasa's climate*

# Malindi – paradise on earth?

From Malindi village down to Watamu lie some gorgeous beaches. Wide sandy stretches backed by dunes or thick casuarina woods, make this Malindi coast quite distinctive.

Underwater, the potato staghorn and mushroom coral are especially beautiful, and the reef off Malindi has been designated a marine reserve.

▲ **D** *Extract from a holiday brochure*

**1** What are the attractions for tourists to Kenya's coastline? Describe four.

## The coral reef

The warm shallow waters of the Indian Ocean have led to the formation, over millions of years, of a coral reef. The reef, which is 1km off-shore, runs almost the whole length of the Kenyan coastline. It provides an amazing underwater experience for scuba divers and snorkellers. People wind-surf in the sheltered waters behind the reef.

Malindi is also the most important big-game fishing centre along the Kenyan coastline. The well-equipped game boats offer a day's fishing in the depths of the Indian Ocean. They head out over the barrier reef to Stork Passage where the largest fish can be found. The peak season is between October and February and a variety of fish can be caught: kingfish, bonito, barracuda, wahoo, tunny, dorado, and marlin.

## Can this paradise survive?

With thousands of visitors flocking to this coastline the delicate ecosystem of its coral reef is now in danger of being severely damaged or even destroyed. In places the coral has already died and the reef is broken. Large numbers of glass-bottomed boats sweep in at low tide, bringing with them scores of tourists – all hoping for a piece of coral or a handful of shells to take home as a souvenir. Large areas have now been roped off to prevent further damage from tourists. Visitors are now confined to exploring areas where the corals have already been damaged, in an attempt to save the rest.

▲ **F** *Coral in the Indian Ocean, off the coast of Kenya*

**2** Why do the coral reefs need to be protected?

**3** Give three ways that the tourists can destroy the coral.

**4** What could happen to the tourist industry if the reefs are not protected?

**5** Imagine you work for the Marine Reserve. Produce a report on Kenya's reef. Describe the reef, what it is like, and where it is; explain how it is being damaged and suggest ideas for protecting the reef.

▼ **E** *The impact of tourism on the reef*

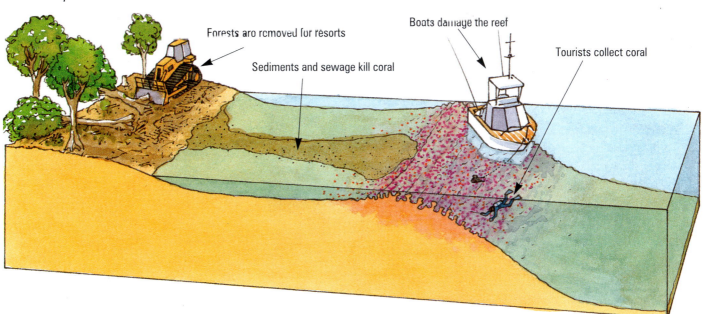

Forests are removed for resorts

Sediments and sewage kill coral

Boats damage the reef

Tourists collect coral

# All in a day's work

Tourism earns a large amount of money for the country but it employs only a small number of people, mainly on the coast. Most Kenyans live and work in rural areas.

## Rural life

As in most African countries, it is the women who do the work in the village – spending hours each day on many back-breaking chores. There is water to carry, crops to tend, and wood to chop and carry back to the village. The supply of wood is essential for survival in a Kenyan village. People use wood in many ways – to cook on their open fires, to build houses, to provide light, and for making toothbrushes.

  Photo A was taken inside an *ola*. These are single-roomed houses built of timber and thatch. They are easily burnt down in cooking accidents. Ware Kiya's *ola* has been burnt down in a cooking accident. Although she has lived in an *ola* all her life, Ware Kiya wishes she could have a stone house to live in.  Her 10-year-old daughter, Dire Kiya, needs somewhere quiet to study in the evenings and both would prefer to have a bathroom within the house.

▼ **A** *The kitchen of a traditional* ola

1 Look carefully at the two photos A and C.
  a) Describe the utensils that you can see by the kitchen fire in photo A.
  b) How does this kitchen compare with your own kitchen? Write down as many similarities and see.
  c) For photo C, how would you describe the load that the two women are carrying?
  d) Describe the area that the two women are walking through to get back to the village.

2 In what ways is the traditional *ola* no longer suited to daily life in the 1990s?

3 Use B.
  a) What percentage of income does the average Kenyan family spend on food?
  b) Describe the main differences between household spending in Kenya and the UK.

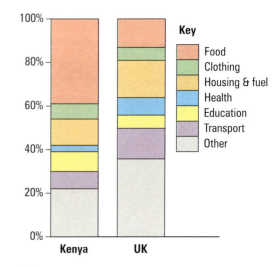

▲ **B** *How household income is spent in Kenya and the UK*

# The need for firewood

◀ **C**
*Christine and Mary returning to the Nkoe homestead with firewood*

The quantities of **firewood** that are needed for the rural population are enormous. Wangari Maathai, formerly professor at Nairobi University, became concerned that the land close to villages would soon become barren and eventually turn to desert. The **deforestation** affects women and children most, as she explains:

'Since women use wood fuel for cooking and they also till the land, my focus was and still is on women. We work together to conserve what is remaining of our environment.'

Wangari Maathai set up a simple tree-planting scheme and made other Kenyans aware of this rapidly developing problem. The project has been a great success; it has a membership of over 50 000 women and about 1500 tree nurseries have been set up. In 22 districts of Kenya over 7 million tree seedlings have already been planted and the remaining 21 districts are planned to be replanted in the next five years.

▼ **D** *Kenya's firewood problem*

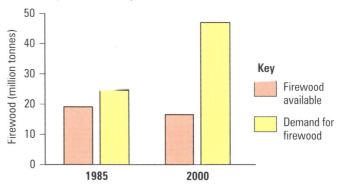

**4** Use graph D to explain Kenya's firewood problem.

**5** What two methods is Wangari Maathai using to help solve the problem?

**6** What do you think the project is trying to achieve?

**7** Discuss Wangari Maathai's statement that deforestation affects women more than men. Explain why this can be true.

# Farming in the savanna

**◄ A** *Goats grazing in the early morning*

**▼ B** *A traditional homestead in the village of Iltilal*

A typical village in the savanna has as many as 200 homesteads. A homestead has a number of single-roomed houses and an enclosure for cattle or goats. Plan B shows the layout of a typical homestead.

Milk is the main food. The land around the village is too dry to grow crops. The animals are moved from place to place to graze. It is important to move on before all the vegetation is eaten and destroyed. Goats will eat anything and so can destroy bushes and small trees that are needed for wood.

Crops can be grown in the wetter parts of Kenya. Maize, wheat, rice, and vegetables are grown to feed Kenya's population. Other crops including avocados, mangoes, and carnations are grown for export and taken by aeroplane to Europe. The most important crops for export are tea and coffee.

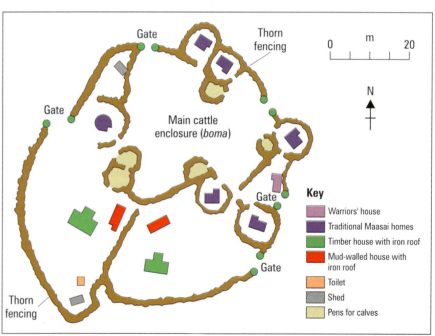

Gate
Thorn fencing
Gate
Gate
Main cattle enclosure (*boma*)
Gate
Gate
Thorn fencing

N

**Key**

- Warriors' house
- Traditional Maasai homes
- Timber house with iron roof
- Mud-walled house with iron roof
- Toilet
- Shed
- Pens for calves

**1** Copy and complete the following:
A savanna village has around 200 ................ Each of these has four or five ............roomed houses and an .................... for the animals.

**2** Explain why the goats have to be grazed carefully.

# Migration to the town

In 1994, 75% of the population lived in rural areas, but many are leaving to live in the city. The number of people living in cities is growing rapidly, as graph C shows.

Farming in the dry savanna regions does not provide enough money for many families to survive. Men have been forced to leave their families, land, and animals to seek work in the city. Some never return or send money back. Many women in the district are left with their children, no money, and in some cases, no food.

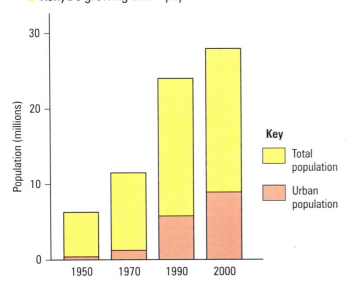

▼ **C** *Kenya's growing urban population*

Many Kenyan women have also been forced to move away from their villages. Although the land is worked by women, it is owned by men. Women are unable to inherit land when their husbands die. Most women in this situation have two choices: they can either work as cheap labour in the village or they can move to the town to find work.

When Maria Mathai's husband died she and her four daughters were left with a small farm on the slopes of Mount Kenya. Although she had worked the land while her husband worked away from home as a sound recordist, she could not continue to farm when her husband died. She was asked to leave the farm by the chief of the village.

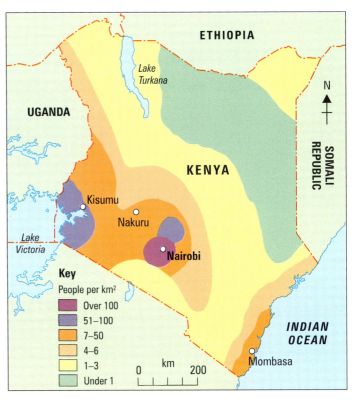

▲ **D** *Map showing* **population density** *in Kenya*

## Improving rural life

A series of projects have been introduced by the government to try to improve life in rural communities. One was the introduction of goats to provide milk for the children of Kibwezi, a village south-east of Nairobi. Bee-keeping has also been introduced and a factory built to refine the honey. This is then sold locally and abroad. Fish farming and rabbit rearing are two other projects within the programme.

**3** Use map D.
  **a)** Which parts of Kenya have least people per km²?
  **b)** What kinds of farming and environment are there in the least populated parts of Kenya? Map A on page 48 will help.

**4** Give reasons why people would want to leave the savanna farmlands. Use these headings: general reasons, why men migrate, why women migrate.

**5** In what ways have people been encouraged to stay in their villages?

## Life in the city

Men and women who move to the cities are looking for work and hoping to build a better life. But is life better in the city? In fact, 70% of Nairobi's 2 million people are now classified as 'urban poor'. They live in the shanty towns on the outskirts of Nairobi. Many of them came from rural villages. The gap between rich and poor continues to get wider because the prices of food and essentials rise faster than the wages of poor people.

▲B *A variety of materials are used to construct simple housing in a shanty town*

Study the two photos A and B carefully.

**1** Pick out of the following list six words/phrases that you think best describe Nairobi: concrete jungle, pleasant surroundings, overcrowded, skyscrapers, flowers and gardens, high-rise buildings, spacious, clean, dirty, modern.

**2** Write a paragraph, including the six words/phrases you have chosen.

**3** Using photo B, list all the different waste materials that have been used to build the house.

**4** Do you think that the shanty houses will last a long time? Suggest what may happen to them eventually.

◀ **C**

*The children make their own recycled goods. They play with hoops and spokes from bicycle wheels, they make matatos (toy trucks) from washing powder tins and bottle tops, and they build go-karts. Anything that the people of Kariobangi cannot use the goats finish off!*

## Recycling for a living in Kariobangi

Kariobangi is a shanty town on the outskirts of Nairobi. It is home to 60 000 people. Some people work in the city but many earn a living locally. There are small craft workshops in Kariobangi and kiosks selling sweets and basic goods. But most people earn their living by turning other people's rubbish into things to sell. Kariobangi is right next door to the rubbish tip where Nairobi's waste is dumped, so the raw materials are on the doorstep.

### Factfile: Recycling

People sort through the rubbish on the tip for items that can be resold, repaired, or manufactured into new goods.

- Margarine tins are made into oil lamps.
- Tomato tins are beaten into flat sheets and used to make briefcases.
- Bracelets are woven from thin strips of plastic.
- Sandals are made from tyres.

Scrap metal is used for making cooking utensils and tools. All containers are recycled: large plastic cooking oil containers are converted to water carriers, with maize cobs used as stoppers.

**5** Make a list of the things that the people of Kariobangi recycle and what they become. Set it out under two column headings: original item, new use.

**6 a)** Look closely at photo C. What items of waste have been used to make this go-kart?

 **b)** Some people regard Kariobangi as a slum. They can find nothing good to say about it. Make up a new caption for photo C. Make it sound as positive as you can. What would you say to people who think Kariobangi is a slum?

**7** Look back to page 55. Imagine that you are one of Maria Mathai's children (about 12 years old). If you had the choice of staying in the village where you were born, on the slopes of Mount Kenya, or moving to the city, which would you choose? What would affect your decision?

# Kenya – a modern trading nation

Kenya is the most industrialized country in East Africa. Industries produce manufactured goods such as textiles, electrical equipment, and shoes, and food products such as coffee, flour, and soft drinks. Over 60% of Kenya's industries are owned by foreign companies which have offices in the high-rise buildings in Nairobi (see photo A, page 56). The city has a good road system and an international airport.

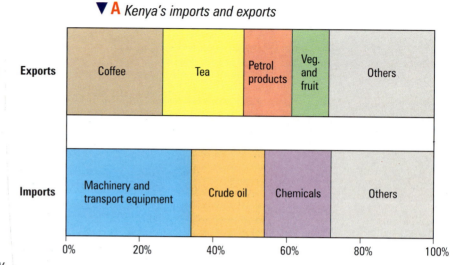

▼ **A** *Kenya's imports and exports*

▼ **B** *The share of wealth created by industry*

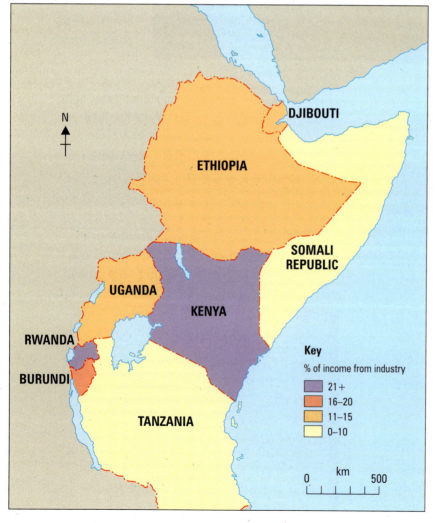

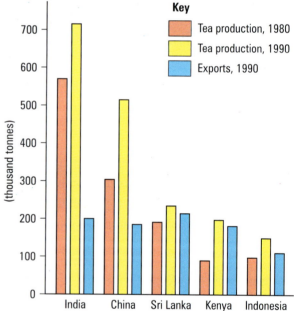

▲ **C** *World tea producers and exporters*

| Country | Tea production | | Exports |
|---------|------|------|------|
| | **1980** | **1990** | **1990** |
| Turkey | 96 | 140 | 28 |
| Bangladesh | 40 | 45 | 27 |
| Malawi | 30 | 43 | 39 |

▲ **D** *Tea production and exports (in thousands of tonnes)*

# The tea trade

▲ **E** *Tea being picked on a Kenyan hillside*

▲ **F** *Tea-growing areas*

**1** Use graph A to copy and complete the following: Kenya's largest export is .......... . Tea comes second with .... % of all exports. Kenya's biggest import is ............... . Crude oil makes up ...% of all imports.

**2** The price of machinery tends to go up faster than the price of tea and coffee. Explain why this would create a problem for Kenya.

**3** Use map B. What is the evidence for the statement that Kenya is the most industrialized country in East Africa? Write a sentence comparing Kenya with two other East African countries.

**4** Use graph C.
**a)** How did tea production change between 1980 and 1990?
**b)** Which two countries exported the largest part of their 1990 crop?
**c)** Kenya is now the world's fourth largest tea producer. Which country has Kenya overtaken?
**d)** Using the information in table D draw a graph in the same style as C for these three countries.

Since 1989 tea production has increased and, unlike most other tea-producing countries, Kenya exports nearly all that it produces. Its tea is of very high quality, which is one reason why demand for it has rapidly increased. In 1990 export earnings from tea were US$273 million. In 1991, Kenyan tea production was over 200000 tonnes. A huge government expansion campaign is now under way so that by the end of the century more than 300000 tonnes of tea will be produced by Kenya.

## Review

Kenya is a successful trading nation. It has taken advantage of its climate, landscape, and wildlife to develop an important tourist industry. Tourism threatens to damage the fragile environments that the visitors come to see, but Kenya is trying to reduce the damage.

Most Kenyans live in rural areas. Rural projects have tried to improve conditions, but many people are moving to the cities to try to find work and a better life.

# **6** Making the most of the weather

In this unit you will study why and how the weather affects us. You will look at how people try to make the best use of the weather and what happens when the weather gets the better of us. By the end of the unit you will be able to explain the difference between weather and climate.

## Why is weather important?

Rain, wind, sunshine, how hot or cold it is, all make up the **weather** we experience every day. The weather affects our lives in many ways. Sporting events like the tennis match in photo B rely on dry weather. The weather can affect the sort of activities we do, the sort of clothes we wear, and where we would like to go for our holiday.

## **Health risks from the cold**

Everyone needs warmth to stay fit and well. If you spend a long time at less than 12°C, there is an increased chance of heart disorder. After a long time at temperatures below 6°C, the system that regulates the body's temperature fails and hypothermia may set in. Those most at risk are elderly people, as they are generally less active; people with restricted mobility, as their circulation may be impaired; and very young babies, because the system which regulates their body temperature has yet to develop.

**1 a)** Working in pairs, describe the weather that you experienced yesterday. These headings may help:
Temperature    Rainfall
Sunshine    Wind.
  **b)** Write a short paragraph explaining how the weather affected what you did yesterday. If the weather had no effect on you, then explain why not.

**2** Read newspaper article A. Which groups of people are most at risk from the cold?

**3** Summarize how the weather would affect two of the following: school sports day, farmers, zoos, electricity and gas supply, water supply, traffic on the motorway.

◀ **A**

◀ **B** *Wimbledon rained off*

# Weather prediction

Changing weather conditions bring their own difficulties. Weather forecasts and predictions are important if we want to avoid the problems that a change in the weather can bring. In most parts of Britain sensors at the roadside like the one in photo E measure air and road temperatures and the amount of moisture on the surface of the road. This information is sent to the highways department who can then send out gritters and snow ploughs when icy conditions are forecast.

▼ **E** *Remote snow and ice sensor*

▼ **C** *Road signs warning of weather hazards*

▼ **D** *Coping with winter weather*

**4 a)** Explain how each of the following weather conditions affects travelling by car: high winds, fog, snow, flooding, bright sunshine, thunderstorms.

**b)** Are some weather conditions more difficult to travel in than others? Categorize the weather conditions into:
- severely affect people travelling
- can affect people travelling
- hardly affect people travelling.

Now explain your choice.

**5** On 9 November 1993, the RAC received 4500 telephone calls an hour from motorists stranded by the snow and freezing conditions.

**a)** Discuss what motorists and their passengers should/should not do if they get stuck in these conditions.

**b)** Devise a poster or leaflet, advising motorists what to take with them in snowy weather, or what to do if they break down.

# People affect the weather

The weather in towns and cities is affected by their buildings. It is usually warmer in the centre of towns than on the outskirts. Heat escapes from the heated buildings. Buildings, roads, and pavements absorb energy from the sun and this re-radiates off and warms the air. For example, in the winter in the centre of London the temperature can be 4°C higher than on the outskirts. This effect is called an **urban heat island**.

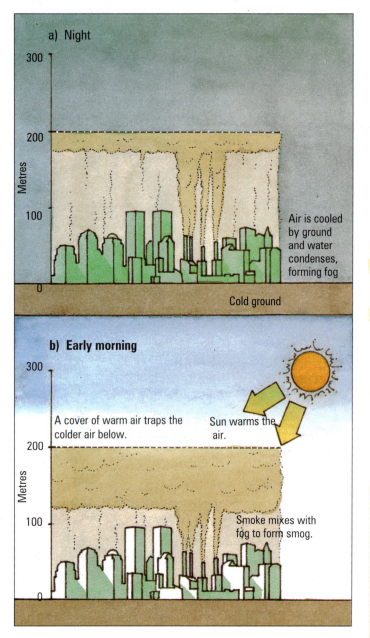

**A** *How smog forms*

# Urban climates and pollution

Heating, exhaust fumes, and industry change the air that we breathe. If it is cold and damp, air pollution, especially from vehicles, mixes with the air to form **smog**. Smog can cause severe problems for people with breathing difficulties. London and Los Angeles suffer from smog. Poor air quality can also build up in the summer when the air does not move around very much. The fumes become trapped as there is no wind to bring fresh air in. When the weather is very sunny, car exhaust fumes react with sunlight to create ozone. This gas irritates the eyes, nose, throat, and lungs. This happened in London in the summer of 1994.

## Smog, I see no smog

Whenever there is still, high-pressure air and long hours of sunshine, traffic will cause pollution levels in and around the capital to lurch upwards. Asthmatics and others with chest illness will wheeze and feel distressed. And motorists will drive on regardless, not giving a hoot.

We can no longer claim ignorance of smog. London and the rest of the country now has a long overdue but half decent air quality monitoring network and pollution forecasting service, making the information available for anyone who wants it.

Weather forecasts in newspapers and on television now warn when poor air quality threatens.

▲ **B** *Extract from* The Independent, *14 July 1994*

1 Use newspaper extract B.
   a) Who suffers most from poor air quality?
   b) How does the air pollution affect people's health?

2 Discuss how the problem of air pollution in urban areas might be solved. Make a list of suggestions in your book.

3 Using diagram A, explain how smog is formed.

## The smog problem in Phoenix, USA

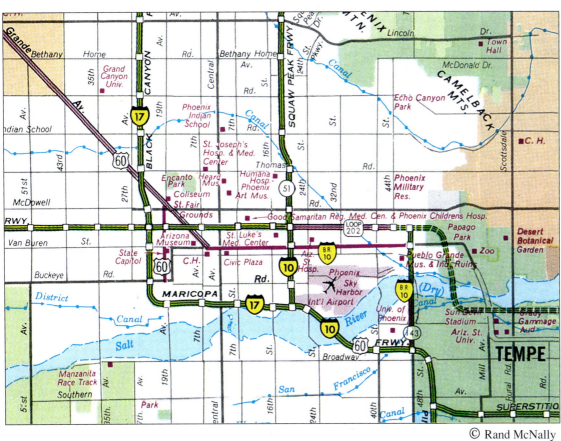

© Rand McNally

Phoenix, USA

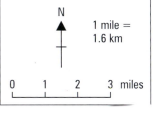

N

1 mile = 1.6 km

0   1   2   3   miles

◀ **C**

*Street map of Phoenix*

▲ **D** *Aerial view of Phoenix*

Phoenix is set in a huge saucer-shaped valley, called the Valley of the Sun. It is a city built for cars. The suburbs stretch for over 80km and the whole city covers an area of over 643 km². With a population of 2.1 million in 1993, the pollution caused by commuters driving to and from work, collects in the valley area and causes smog. Wide-ranging environmental laws are being considered to reduce this pollution.

**4** Look at map C and photo D.
   **a)** Describe the street pattern in Phoenix.
   **b)** What does this tell you about how the city was planned?
   **c)** How does this compare with your local town?

**5** What advantages and disadvantages might there be for people living in Phoenix if the number of cars was reduced? Discuss this with a friend before making a list in your book.

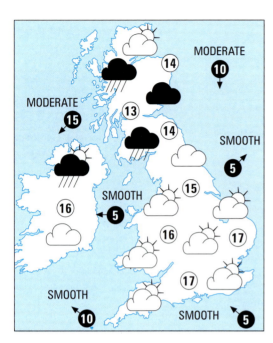

▲ **A** *Weather forecast for 15 October 1994 (taken from* The Guardian*)*

# What is the difference between weather and climate?

There are some parts of the British Isles that, over a year, are drier and warmer than others. The **climate** of Devon and Cornwall is wetter and milder than the climate of north-east Scotland. The climate of an area is the average of the weather over a long period of time, usually 25 or 30 years (see table C). Climate data such as temperature and rainfall are shown on a climate graph, as you can see in graph B.

## A warm autumn in the UK

Day to day weather varies much more than the average climate suggests. November 1994 was the warmest for 300 years. October had also been very mild. On 15 October 1994, temperatures rose to 21°C on the south coast of England and in the Channel Islands. It was like a summer's day. These daily variations in the weather are predicted in weather forecasts like A.

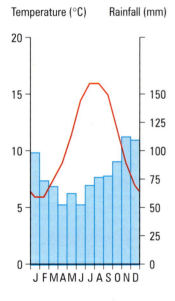

▲ **B** *Climate graph for Plymouth*

| | | Jan | Feb | Mar | Apr | May | Jun | Jul | Aug | Sep | Oct | Nov | Dec |
|---|---|---|---|---|---|---|---|---|---|---|---|---|---|
| Eskdalemuir, Scotland | temp (°C) | 1 | 2 | 4 | 6 | 9 | 11 | 14 | 13 | 11 | 8 | 5 | 3 |
| | rain (mm) | 175 | 112 | 97 | 97 | 87 | 108 | 131 | 120 | 136 | 149 | 153 | 162 |
| London, England | temp (°C) | 4 | 5 | 7 | 8 | 12 | 16 | 18 | 17 | 15 | 11 | 8 | 5 |
| | rain (mm) | 54 | 40 | 37 | 37 | 46 | 45 | 57 | 59 | 49 | 57 | 64 | 48 |
| Aberystwyth, Wales | temp (°C) | 4 | 5 | 6 | 8 | 11 | 13 | 15 | 15 | 13 | 10 | 8 | 6 |
| | rain (mm) | 97 | 72 | 60 | 56 | 65 | 76 | 99 | 93 | 108 | 118 | 111 | 96 |
| Valentia, Ireland | temp (°C) | 7 | 7 | 8 | 10 | 11 | 14 | 15 | 16 | 14 | 11 | 9 | 8 |
| | rain (mm) | 165 | 107 | 103 | 75 | 86 | 81 | 107 | 95 | 122 | 140 | 151 | 168 |

▲ **C** *Climate data for places in the British Isles*

**1 a)** Work in a group of four. Each of you select one of the places in table C and draw a climate graph for that place. Use B to help you. Remember to label the axes and give the graph a title.

**b)** Compare your graph with another one in your group. What similarities and differences do you notice? Write a paragraph comparing your two graphs.

**2** The temperature in Plymouth on 15 October 1994 was 21°C. Using A and B:

**a)** what temperature was forecast for Plymouth?

**b)** how hot is Plymouth normally at this time of year?

**c)** discuss why these temperatures are so different.

# A wet November in Southern Europe

In early November 1994, there was exceptionally heavy rain in northern Italy and southern France. This led to widespread flooding and the deaths of around 90 people. The worst damage was in the Piedmont region of Italy where 500mm of rain fell in just 24 hours. Most of the people died when their cars were swept away in the flood water. Others died when the heavy rain caused **mudslides**. In France, Nice airport was damaged by high winds and torrential rain. Repairs to the airport were estimated to cost £4.1 million.

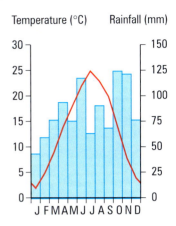

▶ **F** *Climate graph for Milan*

▲ **D** The area affected by the flooding

Hundreds of people were brought to Asti from the countryside after being plucked from the roofs of their homes by helicopters. Most problems were caused by the River Tanaro and its tributary, the Borbone bursting their banks.

Officials denied reports that the flooding was exacerbated when gates of reservoir dams in the mountains of Cuneo province were opened to prevent them bursting under the heavy rainfall.

▲ **G** *Extract adapted from* The Times, *8 November 1994*

**3** Use map D to find out:
   **a)** where is the source of the River Po?
   **b)** in which direction does the River Po flow, and where is its mouth?

**4** Look at graph F:
   **a)** what is the average total amount of rainfall in November?
   **b)** how much more rain fell in just 24 hours, during the November 1994 floods?

**5 a)** Describe the different ways in which the heavy rain and winds caused damage.
   **b)** How might people have made the effects of the flooding worse?

**6** The River Po burst its bank at Pavia, although the rain storm was less severe there. Look at map D, and explain why you think this happened.

**7** Write a brief paragraph for someone younger than yourself explaining the difference between weather and climate.

▲ **E** A woman stands by her gas cooker, next to the ruins of her house

# Using the weather to generate electricity

Harnessing the power of the wind is not a new idea. For over 2000 years the wind has propelled ships across the oceans, powered mills to process food, and pumped water to drive machinery.

Wind energy is once again being harnessed, this time to generate electricity. As we use up more and more oil, coal, and gas we are looking for types of energy that will not run out. These are known as **renewable** or alternative energy sources. These sources of energy are described as environmentally friendly.

**Factfile: Alternative energy sources**

Alternative energy sources should:

● be renewable

● produce little or no pollution or waste

● have little visual impact on the landscape and create little noise

● not disturb wildlife or protected landscapes.

▲ **B** *A modern wind farm*

Wind turbines, as in photo B, are a good example of an alternative energy source. The best sites are the windiest ones (see map A). Where several wind turbines are grouped together they are called wind farms. Delabole wind farm, 3km inland from the North Cornwall coast, was the first commercial wind farm in the British Isles. It has ten wind turbines, the first of which started operation in December 1991.

**1 a)** On an outline map or tracing of Great Britain mark the windiest areas.

**b)** Use an atlas to name the areas.

**c)** Are any of the windy areas in National Parks? If they are, colour these areas red. Colour the remaining areas green. Give your map a suitable key.

**d)** Using the map you have drawn, decide which areas are most suitable for building wind farms. Explain your answer.

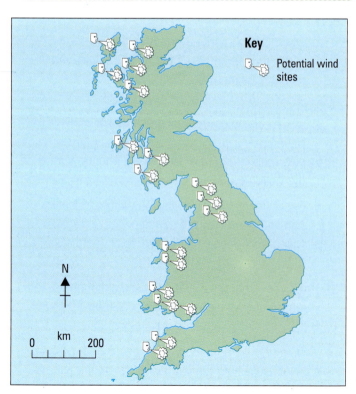

**Key**

🏠🌀 Potential wind sites

N

km
0    200

▲ **A** *The windiest parts of Great Britain*

## Are wind farms a good idea?

Not everyone agrees that wind farms are a good idea. The letters in C were written during the planning stage of a Welsh wind farm. The District Council received 145 letters in total: 35 objecting to the scheme, and 110 letters of support.

▼ **C** *Extracts from letters sent to Montgomery District Council about the proposed Cemmaes Road wind farm*

(i)
> The number, size, and location of windmills proposed are such that the site would stick out like a sore thumb (or a very large number of sore thumbs) not only when viewed from the valley itself, but also when seen from the hills from many miles around.

(ii)
> The beauty of our undeveloped countryside is our main tourist attraction.

(iii)
> I was on holiday in Denmark last year and noticed many larger wind turbines than the ones proposed here. Denmark is very flat and the turbines were highly visible, but they seemed to be very graceful when turning slowly in the wind.

(iv)
> The only significant effects are visual impact and noise. Both are very localized ... the noise should be completely inaudible from the nearest building.

(v)
> Wind farms create far less environmental impact than the alternatives of fossil fuel or nuclear power generation.

(vi)
> Although I live in the Midlands, I spend much of the summer months near Bala and spend my time hill walking. A wind farm would be a visual blight on the landscape and would ruin the view from several peaks including Cader Idris and the Arans.

(vii)
> The development should create jobs and help the local economy in an area where the government is trying to encourage upland farmers to diversify.

(viii)
> A grant to insulate my roof might be a cheaper way of saving energy.

The Cemmaes wind farm was eventually built, but it has run into problems, as you can see from D.

▼ **D** *Extract adapted from* The Times*, 24 December 1993*

### Gales too strong for wind farm

Winds of over 160 kph have closed three of Britain's biggest wind farms. On the nights of 8, 9, and 10 December three turbines broke at Cemmaes wind farm, Powys. The wind farm, which cost £9 million to build and has 24 wind turbines, was opened last year. A fourth turbine broke on 19 December.

**2** Read through the extracts in C.
   a) Decide whether each extract is for or against building the wind farm. Make two lists in your book.
   b) Decide which of the following arguments each extract is really using:
   • impact on the local environment
   • impact on the local people and jobs
   • impact on the wider environment.

**3** Imagine you were the planning officer who received the letters. What would you recommend should happen?

**4** Using all the resources on these pages, do you think that wind farms meet the requirements for alternative energy sources given in the factfile?

# Dramatic weather events

The climatic conditions of some places give rise to severe weather conditions. Fierce storms occur in tropical areas during late summer or early autumn. These storms have different names in different continents: hurricanes in North America, **cyclones** in the Bay of Bengal, and typhoons in south-east Asia.

Tropical storms are one of the most powerful weather systems on earth. They produce:
- winds that reach up to 160kph
- heavy rain storms with huge amounts of thunder and lightning
- strong winds which create enormous waves. These drive water far inland. They are called **storm surges**.

About 90% of deaths during tropical storms are caused by the storm surge.

## How tropical storms are formed

Tropical storms start out at sea. This is how they develop:

1 Warm moist air rises from the ocean.
2 Air rushes in over the ocean to replace it, producing violent winds and waves.
3 As the warm air rises it cools and condenses, leading to heavy rainfall.
4 The storm spins its way towards the land, gaining strength and ferocity as it goes.
5 It loses energy over land, because there is no supply of warm water to drive the system.

## Tropical storms (typhoons) in Hong Kong

Typhoons can hit Hong Kong any time between July and November. The word typhoon comes from the Chinese *tai fung*, meaning the big wind.

There are over 6 million people living in Hong Kong. Typhoon warnings on a scale from 1 to 10 are given out on the radio and the television. In 1993 there were four T8 warnings. One of these was Typhoon Dot which caused floods up to 7m deep in some places. Another was Typhoon Ira (see source C).

▲ **A** *Storm surge on the coast of Miami, Florida, 1948*

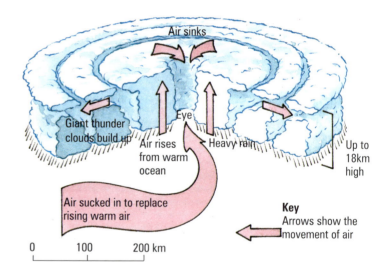

▲ **B** *Cross-section through a tropical storm*

# Typhoon Ira hits Hong Kong

Rain associated with Ira was quite exceptional. More than 700mm fell on the western part of Hong Kong on November 4th and 5th 1993. There were extensive landslides on Lantau island and widespread flooding in Tuen Mun and Yuen Long. Burst water mains on Cheung Chau island resulted in a cut-off of fresh water supply for four days.

▲ **C** *Extract from* Hong Kong Year Book, *1994*

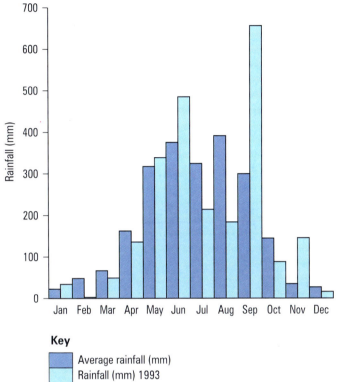

◀ **D** *Landslides often occur in Hong Kong after the heavy rainfall*

**Key**

Average rainfall (mm)
Rainfall (mm) 1993

▲ **E** *Rainfall for 1993 compared with average rainfall in Hong Kong*

**1** Copy diagram B and label it using the section 'How tropical storms are formed'.

**2** What are the features of tropical storms that make them so dangerous?

**3** Prepare a typhoon warning for Hong Kong to be given out on the radio. Describe the sort of weather that it will bring and how long it will last.

**4** Study rainfall graph E.
   **a)** What is the average rainfall in November?
   **b)** How much more rain fell in November 1993 than the average for the month?
   **c)** Typhoon Dot hit Hong Kong in the autumn. Use the graph to find out in which month it happened.

**5** Use what you have learnt about Hong Kong to explain the difference between weather and climate.

# Review

- **Weather** is the amount of sun, wind, and rain that we experience each day.
- **Climate** is the weather experienced in a place over a number of years. Records are kept day by day and an average worked out after 20 or 30 years.
- Both weather and climate have a direct influence on the way we live – how we travel, what we wear, what farmers grow.

By understanding the climate for different places we can make the best use of it, for example by putting wind farms in windy places.

# Pressures on the Mediterranean

The Mediterranean Sea is the shallow sea that separates Europe from Africa. The Mediterranean region includes the coastal areas of nineteen countries in southern Europe and northern Africa. How have changes in farming, tourism, and industry created problems for the region? What damage has been done to the environment? How can the region continue to develop without further damage being caused?

▼ **A** *Pollution in the Mediterranean*

The Mediterranean Sea is almost completely surrounded by land. It is connected to the much larger Atlantic Ocean at its western end by the narrow Strait of Gibraltar. The Mediterranean has practically no **tide**. This has advantages for tourists who can sit by the water's edge without having to move up and down the beach! However, it also means that the beaches are not cleaned by the tide, and popular tourist beaches would become very dirty if they were not swept.

**1** Using map A:
   **a)** how many African countries have Mediterranean coasts?
   **b)** how long is the Mediterranean from east to west?
   **c)** which two parts of the sea are the most heavily polluted by farming?

# Polluting the Mediterranean Sea

The coast attracts many people to live and work in the region. About 370 million people now live in the region. Each year as many as 200 million tourists add to the numbers, and increase the pressure on the environment. Holidaymakers use five to six times as much water each day as the local residents, and create enormous amounts of waste. As much as 85% of the sewage pumped into the Mediterranean is untreated.

▼ **B** *Cleaning the beach*

Evidence shows that much of the area's marine pollution originates on land: from domestic and industrial waste water, agricultural run-off, the inadequate disposal of solid waste, and discharges from ships and shipping accidents. As population increases and urban areas spread, these land-based problems worsen.

▲ **C** *Extract from* World Bank Information Brief, *April 1994*

## Industrial and agricultural waste

The rivers which pour into the sea contain waste from factories, and chemical fertilizers and pesticides that have been washed off farm land by rain water. Every year 1.5 million tonnes of waste chemicals pollute the sea. Ships carry hundreds of tonnes of crude oil across the sea each year. An oil spill in 1991 spilled 55 million litres of oil on the French coast. The waste cannot easily escape, as diagram D shows.

▼ **D** *How pollution builds up*

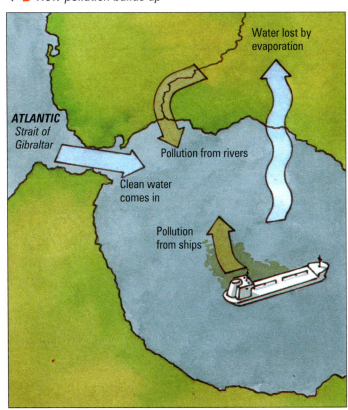

**2** List three types of pollution that enter the sea.

**3** Why is it particularly important to keep the beaches clean? Consider the tide, health, and the impact on tourism in your answer.

**4** Using C, does most waste seem to come from rivers or from ships?

**5** Make a copy of diagram D. Use it to explain why the pollution gets trapped.

# People and wildlife compete for space

The millions of people who live in and visit the region are creating problems for the environment. New towns and resorts pollute the sea and threaten wildlife. The rare loggerhead turtle still lives in the eastern part of the region but is in danger.

The small Greek island of Zakynthos has the largest known rookery of loggerhead turtles in the Mediterranean. Every year there are about 2000 turtle nests on the island. In mid-June the female turtles dig holes in the sand and lay their eggs. The eggs lie in the sand until mid-August. The young hatch out at night and scamper down the beach into the sea where they are safe from rats and gulls.

▲ **B** *The endangered loggerhead turtle*

## The growth of tourism threatens the turtles

Greece has become a popular holiday destination. The hot dry summers and sandy beaches are the main attractions. Some visitors come to Zakynthos especially to see the turtles.

During the day tourists trample on the nesting beaches and unknowingly stamp on buried eggs. Turtle watching at night also frightens the animals and prevents nesting.

▼ **A** *The eastern part of the Mediterranean region*

Key
■ Main turtle breeding areas

Istanbul

GREECE

TURKEY

Athens

Zakynthos

Dalyan

CYPRUS

Crete

MEDITERRANEAN SEA

N

km
0    300

# Dalyan. Outstanding natural beauty and relaxed Turkish charm

Surrounded by pine-clad hills, cotton fields, and bulrushes, Dalyan really is a beautiful place. The village is in the centre of a broad delta, at the head of which is a sandbar of fine, gently shelving sands known as Iztuzu Beach. The endangered loggerhead turtle has returned here for hundreds of years and this is now a conservation area. The beach has also become a haven for the fortunate sunseekers who have discovered this relatively unspoilt corner of Turkey.

▲ **C** *Extract from holiday brochure*

◀ **D** *Turtle beach at Dalyan*

We've worked with local people to make them aware of the problems the turtles have. On three beaches sand was being removed to use on a building site for a new hotel. This has now stopped.

Another hotel has put up screens so that lights from the windows do not confuse the turtles on the beach.

Barriers have been built to prevent cars from driving on other beaches, and tourists can only visit the beach at night in small guided groups.

▲ **E** *A conservationist with the World Wide Fund for Nature (WWF) explains how the turtles are protected*

WWF is currently operating 25 major conservation projects in the Mediterranean, informing tourists and sponsoring scientific study.

For instance, on the Majorcan reserve of La Trapa, rare falcons, eagles and 150 plant species – including 16 different types of orchid – are now protected by WWF. But other species are not so lucky. The Mediterranean monk seal population has been reduced to under 1000. They are killed by fishermen as competitors for fish stocks, and available habitat has been greatly reduced because of coastal development, especially tourism.

▲ **F** *Extract from World Wide Fund for Nature (WWF) newsletter*

## Can tourism and the environment work together?

The people of Zakynthos, and communities like them, need the jobs and money that tourism creates. They also need to protect the landscape and wildlife. If the resorts grow too fast, and the environment is spoilt, the tourists may stop coming.

**1** Which Mediterranean countries have loggerhead turtles?

**2** Using C and D, list the main attractions of a holiday in this part of the Mediterranean.

**3** How do tourists threaten the turtles? You might consider what you learned on pages 70–71, as well as the information on this page.

**4** Imagine you are on holiday in Dalyan. You have been to see the turtles hatching out. Write a postcard home describing what it was like. Use C, D, and E for ideas.

**5** *Imagine a conversation between a hotel developer, a tourist, a local barman, and a conservationist from the World Wide Fund for Nature. Discuss what they might say about building a new hotel in Dalyan. Write a summary of your discussion.*

# The Mediterranean environment

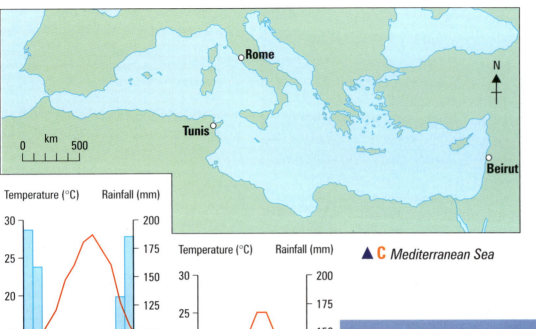

Temperature (°C)    Rainfall (mm)

▲ **A** *Climate graph for Rome*

▶ **B** *Climate graph for Tunis*

Temperature (°C)    Rainfall (mm)

▲ **C** *Mediterranean Sea*

Temperature (°C)    Rainfall (mm)

▲ **D** *Climate graph for Beirut*

You can see from the climate graphs why so many people are attracted to the region. The Mediterranean has hot dry summers. The winters are cooler but still warm. Most rain falls in the autumn and winter.

This climate helps to give the Mediterranean region its own distinctive environment. The landscape is rocky with thin soil and covered by low shrubby plants or scrub. These plants are adapted to the dry environment. The Mediterranean climate and vegetation can also be found in other parts of the world such as California in the USA, southern Australia, and South Africa.

Plants are evergreen. They grow best when the weather is cool and damp

Very thin soils on the limestone rock

Plants grow in crevices where they are shaded from the sun and where some soil builds up from leaf litter

Small leaves and woody stems cut down water loss by transpiration

▲ **E** *Typical Mediterranean plants on Menorca, Spain*

## Why are there so few trees?

In other parts of the Mediterranean, cork oak and pine trees grow. These trees are evergreens with small leaves. They were once more common, but people have lived in this region for thousands of years, and many forests have been cut down. This process of **deforestation** still continues in places like Tunisia.

In rural Tunisia wood fires are used to bake bread. Wood smoke fills the single-roomed houses during winter. Often there is no chimney and the whole family is affected by smoke. The stove uses only 10% of the wood's energy. The rest is wasted. The following suggestions were made as the result of a study.

- Bread could be baked on a shared village stove. The design of the stove could also be improved. This would reduce the amount of wood used by 50%.
- Grazing by goats in forested areas should be stopped as they stunt the growth of young trees.
- Trees must be planted to replace the ones that have been lost.

### Gobbling up the forests

In the mountainous areas of north-west Tunisia, women spend three to four hours a day collecting firewood. Every year each family burns 4.5 tonnes of wood just to bake bread. The magnificent pine and cork oak forests have declined by over 40% in the last 40 years. The shrinking of the forest cover has accelerated soil erosion and caused underground water sources to dry up, seriously affecting the country's agriculture. Commercial logging, overgrazing of livestock, and firewood collection are all to blame.

▲ **F** *Extract adapted from* The Power to Change *by Essma Ben Hamida, 1992*

**1 a)** Copy and complete the following. Scrub vegetation is common in the Mediterranean region. Plants have to be ............ to the climate which is ...... and ..... in the summer months.

**b)** Finish these notes on vegetation by listing ways in which plants cope with the climate.

**2** Look at A, B and D. Which city is hottest in June? What other differences can you see between the three graphs?

**3 a)** Draw a divided bar or pictograph to show how much forest has been lost in Tunisia.

**b)** List the reasons for the deforestation.

**c)** Explain how the new stoves will help to solve the problem.

**4** *Research through the book to write a report on deforestation. Units 1, 3, and 5 all have useful information in them. The report should include:*

*a) where deforestation is happening*

*b) why it is happening*

*c) what can be done to prevent it.*

► **G**

*Herding sheep and goats in Tunisia*

# Farming in the Mediterranean region

The hot dry summers create problems for people as well as for plants. Farming, industry, tourism, and local people all use water, which is in short supply for much of the year. Farmers in the Mediterranean have always had to cope with a lack of water. Olives and grapes are two traditional crops that can survive the long hot summer. Olive trees grow happily in poor soils. Their deep roots can get to water deep underground.

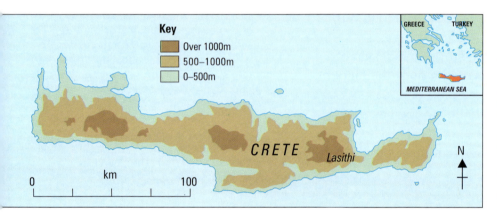

▲ **A** *The island of Crete*

## Traditional farming in Crete

Crete is a mountainous Greek island in the eastern Mediterranean. Rivers have cut down deeply into the mountains forming deep gorges. Soils are thin and the slopes are bare and rocky. The land is dry and the rainfall unreliable. Much of the south coast has no roads. It is easier to reach some southern villages by sea than by land. As in the rest of the Mediterranean, water is a key issue.

In the Lasithi Plain in eastern Crete, windmills help solve the water problem. Ground water is pumped to the surface by windmills that are dotted all over the plain. The water **irrigates** crops of olives, lemons, figs, and almonds. The windmills are a good answer to the water problem. They are cheap to run and easy to look after.

1 Copy and complete the following.
............ is the biggest producer of olives in the world with .......%. It is also the first/second/third largest producer of wine. The Mediterranean region produces over .....% of the world's wine.

2 Draw a pie chart similar to that in B to show olive production.

3 Draw a sketch map of Crete. Label your map with reasons why farming is difficult in particular parts of the island.

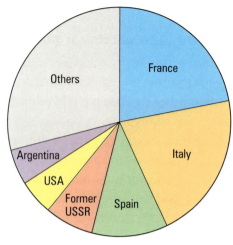

▲ **B** *Wine producers*

| Production | | |
|---|---|---|
| **Country** | **%** | **Tonnes (thousands)** |
| Italy | 31 | 3250 |
| Spain | 27 | 2891 |
| Greece | 17 | 1800 |
| Turkey | 8 | 800 |
| Morocco | 4 | 440 |
| Tunisia | 3 | 330 |
| | | |

▲ **C** *World olive production*

▲ **D** *The water windmills of Lasithi*

## Increasing demands for the water resource

The Languedoc, in the French part of the Mediterranean region, produces 40% of all French wine. However, soils in the Languedoc are poor and so are the grapes. The wine that is produced is sold very cheaply as *vin ordinaire* (table wine) for as little as 4 francs (50p) a litre in French supermarkets. The rest is converted into alcohol for use by industry.

Some farmers have dug up their vines and are now growing vegetables and soft fruit such as strawberries, artichokes, peaches, apricots, and tomatoes. These crops are more valuable, but they need more water to grow properly in this dry region. Photo F shows rows of apricot trees growing in the Languedoc.

Modern **irrigation** methods can be very wasteful. Often, water is sprayed from a jet or revolving sprinkler. In both cases a lot of water is lost by evaporation. Farmers need to be given training about how to grow the new crops. This training is paid for by the European Union. The new crops also need more chemical fertilizers and pesticides than the vines. These chemicals are washed into rivers, and then pollute the sea.

▲ **F** *Apricot trees growing in the dry soil of the Languedoc*

**4** Explain why modern irrigation methods can be very wasteful of water.

**5** Explain why the new crops create more problems for the environment than the vines.

**6** Refer back to page 70. Which parts of the Mediterranean are worst affected by nitrates from fertilizer run-off? Use the map to work out which countries are probably to blame for this pollution.

► **E** *The Languedoc region of France*

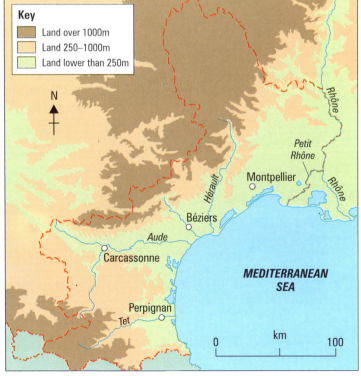

Key
- Land over 1000m
- Land 250–1000m
- Land lower than 250m

# Complex problems – complex solutions

The Italian city of Venice sums up the complex issues facing the Mediterranean today. Italy attracts over 50 million tourists every year. Three million people come to Venice and the nearby beaches. They admire the beautiful buildings and art galleries or ride on one of the city's canals, as you can see in photo B. Venice is built on wooden piles driven into the soft muds of the River Po delta. It is slowly sinking into the polluted waters of the Mediterranean. The visitors help to create wealth and jobs, but they also create waste and pollution problems for the city. It will take a massive effort to save the city, and an international effort to save the Mediterranean.

▲ **B** *The canals and historic buildings of Venice*

▼ **A** *False-colour satellite image of Venice*

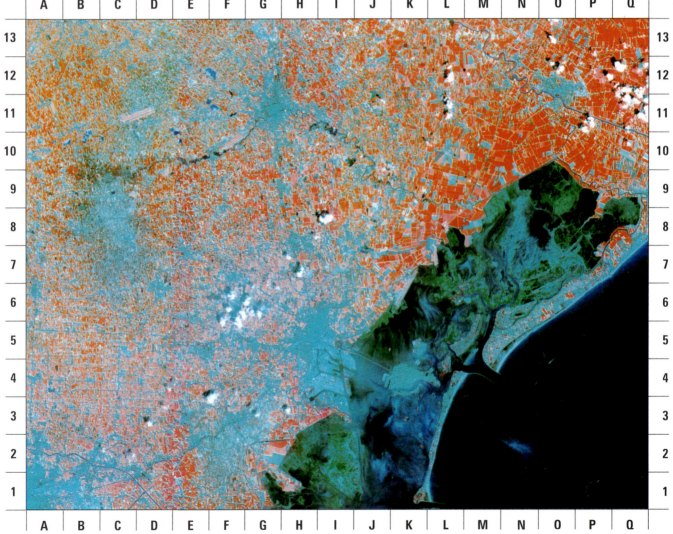

© CNES/SPOT Image

Fields can be clearly seen in shades of red and pink. Nitrates from fertilizers run off into the sea.

Water shows as blue. The deeper water almost black. Very shallow water shows lighter blue because of reflections off the sand beneath.

Green areas in the sea are areas of foul-smelling seaweed. The seaweed grows well because it is fed by nitrates from fertilizers on the fields and phosphates from sewage.

The built-up area of the city and roads show as blue/turquoise.

# The future of the Mediterranean region

The Mediterranean faces serious problems, as map C suggests. If these problems are going to be solved, it will take international co-operation. In 1990 the countries of the European Union got together with the United Nations and the World Bank to draw up a new plan to save the Mediterranean. This plan includes:

- control of industrial waste from Egypt
- management of developments along the Turkish coast and control of pollution
- study and conservation of wildlife and plants of the whole region.

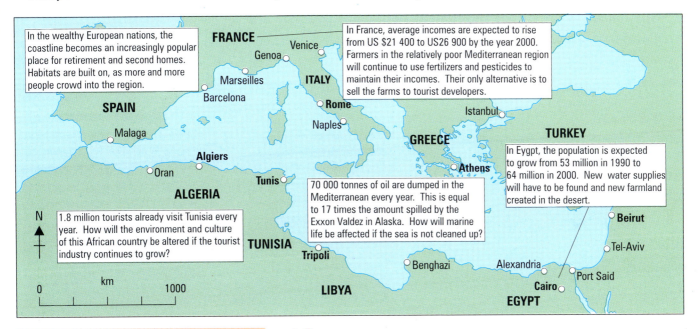

In the wealthy European nations, the coastline becomes an increasingly popular place for retirement and second homes. Habitats are built on, as more and more people crowd into the region.

In France, average incomes are expected to rise from US \$21 400 to US26 900 by the year 2000. Farmers in the relatively poor Mediterranean region will continue to use fertilizers and pesticides to maintain their incomes. Their only alternative is to sell the farms to tourist developers.

In Eygpt, the population is expected to grow from 53 million in 1990 to 64 million in 2000. New water supplies will have to be found and new farmland created in the desert.

1.8 million tourists already visit Tunisia every year. How will the environment and culture of this African country be altered if the tourist industry continues to grow?

70 000 tonnes of oil are dumped in the Mediterranean every year. This is equal to 17 times the amount spilled by the Exxon Valdez in Alaska. How will marine life be affected if the sea is not cleaned up?

▲ **C** *Issues facing the Mediterranean region*

**1** Make a sketch or tracing of photo B. Label it with the features that tourists would find attractive.

**2** Look back at photo D on page 73. In what way is Venice different from other resorts?

**3** Study the satellite image and its labels carefully.
**a)** Give a grid reference for each of the following features: fields, deep water, shallow water and sand, seaweed.
**b)** Draw a sketch of Venice. Label the shallow water of the lagoon and shade in the most polluted parts. Write a paragraph under your sketch explaining where the pollution has come from.

## Review

The Mediterranean region is the most popular tourist destination in the world. The region has its own distinctive climate and vegetation. Population growth, farming, tourism, and industry all create waste and pollution problems. These activities also make demands on water and land resources.

International attempts are being made to save the Mediterranean, but so far they have had only limited success.

**4** *Study map C. Imagine you are working with the United Nations. Discuss which problems would have your priority.*

**5** *Why is it particularly difficult to solve international problems like the one in the Mediterranean?*

# 8 Spain

Spain is a Mediterranean country that illustrates many of the issues that we saw in Unit 7, such as the impact of tourism and demand for water. Spain is a country full of contrasts. What is Spain like? What are the differences between Andalusia and Catalonia? How has Spain developed?

► **A** Tourists on the Costa del Sol

▼ **B** Spain

**Key**
Height of the land (m)

| | |
|---|---|
| ▮ | 2000–4000 |
| ▮ | 1000–2000 |
| ▮ | 400–1000 |
| ▮ | 200–400 |
| ▮ | 0–200 |
| | Sea level |

N

0  100  200  300
km

ATLANTIC OCEAN

Bay of Biscay

FRANCE

UK

La Coruña

Cantabrian Mountains

Bilbao

Pyrenees

Pico de Aneto 3404

Ebro

Duero

Valladolid

Zaragoza

CATALONIA

Costa Brava

Barcelona

PORTUGAL

Madrid

Tajo

SPAIN

Valencia

BALEARIC ISLANDS

Lisbon

Sierra Morena

Guadalquivir

Murcia

Costa Blanca

Seville

Granada

Sierra Nevada

ANDALUSIA

Costa del Sol

Gibraltar (UK)

MEDITERRANEAN

ALGERIA

MOROCCO

## What is Spain like?

Spain is one of the most rapidly changing countries in Europe. In the 1940s, 52% of the Spanish people worked in farming. It was seen as a poor or developing country. Agriculture now produces only 5% of Spain's wealth and employs 10% of its workforce. Spain's hot dry climate has helped to make tourism its most important industry. Spain is the eighth biggest **economy** in the world, but with 20% of its workers unemployed it also has the highest unemployment rate in the European Union.

The landscape is very varied, with long sandy beaches but with high plains and mountains beyond the coast. The Pyrenees in the north and the Sierra Nevada in the south rise to over 3000m in height, and the centre of the country is dominated by a vast highland called the Meseta. Much of Spain is hot and gets little rainfall, but the north and north-west are more humid.

## Tourism

Spain is the most popular tourist destination in the world. The country has a population of 39 million people but it is visited each year by over 50 million holidaymakers. Tourism employs 11% of Spanish workers. The country makes more money from tourism than any other country in the world. Map C shows the importance of tourism in each region of Spain.

▼ **C** *The importance of tourism to the regions of Spain*

**Area:** 504 780 km²

**Population:** 39 200 000

**Capital:** Madrid (population 3.1 million)

**Major imports:** Machinery and electrical equipment (20%), fuels and petroleum products (19%), chemicals (9%)

**Major exports:** Cars and car parts (17%), machinery and electrical equipment (13%), vegetables and fruit (9%)

**GNP:** US $12 460 per person

1 Using map B and the factfile, copy and complete the following:
Spain is in SW Europe. It shares borders with .......... to the west, and France to the .......... The capital city is ..........

2 Measure the distance:
**a)** from Madrid to Barcelona
**b)** along the Mediterranean coastline.

3 Why do you think Spain is so popular with tourists? Think of as many reasons as you can.

4 Using maps B and C, describe the location of the most popular tourist resorts in Spain.

▼ **D** *Madrid, the capital city*

# Cheap holidays for all?

The mild winter climate and the hot dry summers of the Mediterranean region attract millions of visitors every year. Italy and Spain were the first to develop package holidays in the 1950s and 1960s. For the first time people were offered their flight, accommodation, and meals in a single price package. Shopping for a holiday has become very easy. You can now buy your holiday like anything else, from a catalogue or from your local travel agent. Cheap flights and package holidays have made holidays in the sun affordable for many.

1 Use photos A and B.
  a) List the differences you can see.
  b) Describe how the growth of tourism has affected the coastal area.

2 a) How hot is Almeria in January?
  b) Describe the pattern of rainfall through the year.

▲ **A** *The fishing village of Benidorm before the resort was developed*

◄ **C**
*Climate of Almeria, Costa del Sol*

▶ **B** *The resort of Benidorm today*

## Different holidays – different tourists

Not everyone wants a holiday on one of the hot Mediterranean beaches. Some people also want to get away from the crowds, and organize their own holiday. Many people visit Spain's historic cities such as Madrid, Córdoba, and Seville. Others travel to Spain by car or ferry and visit the Atlantic coastline of northern Spain, as shown in photo E, where the climate is wetter and cooler. Other people visit Spain in the winter, to take advantage of the warm winter weather, as extract D shows.

▼ **D** *Extract adapted from* The Sunday Times, *30 October 1988*

▲ **E** *The coastline of Galicia, northern Spain*

# Retiring from the cool British winter

The over-55s, in return for having to bear such jazzy labels as Woopies (Well-Off Older People) and Jollies (Jet-setting Oldies with Lots of Loot), at least enjoy an enormous range of travel options. With a third of the UK population now over 55, the market is twice as important to the tour operators as the more publicized 18–30s.

Among the best bargains on offer this winter are long-stay holidays, lasting from 28 days to 6 months. Prices are extremely low. The other advantage of long-stay holidays is the money saved on home outgoings, especially domestic heating costs (which average about £10 per person per week) and food.

| Country of origin | Number of nights stayed (millions) by resort | | | |
|---|---|---|---|---|
| | Balearics | Madrid | Malaga | Tenerife |
| Spain | 9.2 | 3.8 | 6.4 | 3.6 |
| UK | 8.8 | – | 1.4 | 3.0 |
| Germany | 12.2 | – | 0.6 | 1.4 |
| France | 3.2 | – | 1.0 | 0.8 |
| Others | 6.4 | 3.0 | 2.8 | 2.1 |

▲ **F** *Different resorts attract people from different countries. The figures show the number of nights (in millions) spent in hotels in August 1990*

**3** Using the newspaper extract D, explain what the advantages are for winter tourists.

**4** Compare photos B and E.
  a) Describe the differences you can see.
  b) Discuss the kinds of holidays the following people might like in Spain:
   (i) a family with young children
   (ii) a party of young single people
   (iii) an older couple without children.

c) Suggest which resort the people in **b)** may want to visit, B, E, or some other place. Give reasons for your answer.

**5** a) Using F, describe the differences you can see between the resorts.
  b) Why do you think people from the UK and Germany are particularly attracted to the Mediterranean resorts?

# Contrasting regions

Spain is made up of seventeen regions, which are known as communities. Their landscape, climate, culture, language, and wealth vary a great deal. Recently Spain has become much wealthier yet it still has some of the poorest areas in the European Union.

Changes in farming, the development of tourism, and the growth of new industries have happened only in some regions, others are suffering great problems.

## Spain's four contrasting regions

Spain can be divided into four economic regions that show how uneven Spain's development has been.

◀ **A** *The four economic regions of Spain*

1 **Growing Spain**
- Lots of new jobs in service industries
- Specialized farming
- Modern industry

2 **Spain in crisis**
- Old industrial areas now in decline
- Steel plants and coal mines have closed down
- Increasing unemployment

3 **Unchanging Spain**
- No new industry
- Farms still grow traditional crops such as olives and cereals
- Underdeveloped

4 **Shrinking Spain**
- Large numbers of people moving out of the area
- High percentage of elderly people
- Little work
- Mountainous landscape makes farming difficult

**Key**
- Growing Spain
- Spain in crisis
- Unchanging Spain
- Shrinking Spain

0 km 200

**Key**

GNP per person
- 14 000–15 999
- 12 000–13 999
- 10 000–11 999
- 8 000–9 999

0 km 200

◀ **B** *Variations in wealth in Spain*

**1** Summarize the main strengths and weaknesses of the four different parts of Spain under the following headings:
Population   Industry   Farming.

**2** What is the average income in:
**a)** Andalusia   **b)** Catalonia   **c)** Balearics?

**3** What are the similarities and differences between maps A and B? Concentrate on the regions of Catalonia and Andalusia.

**4 a)** Which parts of Spain are growing?
**b)** How do these areas compare with the tourism map C on page 81?

# Andalusia – Spain's poorest region

Tourism employs 60% of the working population of Andalusia and is the most important source of income for the region. Agriculture is the next biggest earner. However, unemployment is high and the average income is very low. Andalusia is one of the least developed areas of Spain.

The landscape varies from long sandy beaches to high mountains and desert. The desert has been used to film Westerns and 'Wild West' style towns have been built. Farming is important to the region and new methods and new crops have been introduced. Flowers, fruit, and vegetables of all kinds are grown in plastic greenhouses, as you can see in photo C. In Almeria these cover 10 000 hectares and produce 250 million kilograms of crops a year. Most of these are exported to other European countries.

▲ **C** Strawberries growing in plastic greenhouses

▲ **D** Industrial Spain

▲ **E** Andalusia, Spain

The River Guadalquivir flows through Andalusia. Its source is in the mountains where it is fed by relief rainfall. It travels nearly 700 km to the Atlantic Ocean, where it forms a delta 160 km wide. Very little rain falls in the delta. Both farming and tourism depend on water, either from the river or stored underground. The demand for water is so great that it has be transferred 1025 km from the River Tajo in the mountains close to Madrid to Murcia, Alicante, and Almeria.

**5 a)** Why does water have to be transferred from other parts of Spain to Andalusia?
**b)** Who are the main users of water?

## Coto de Doñana

The growth of agriculture and tourism is vital for the region. Both need water, a precious resource in this arid region, and so they are in direct conflict with each other. The environment is also threatened by the development of these industries.

▼ **A** *Map extract of southern Spain showing the River Guadalquivir and Coto de Doñana at 1: 400 000*

▲ **B**

*The imperial eagle*

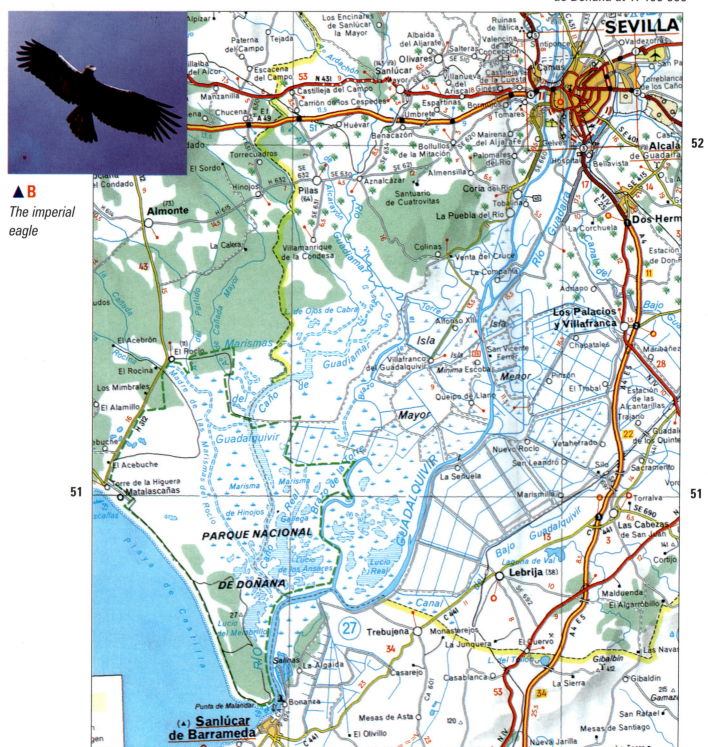

**1** Use map A.
  **a)** What town is at the mouth of the Guadalquivir?
  **b)** Calculate the size of the Doñana National Park (the area edged in green). How big is this compared with the total wetland area: 25%, 50%, or 100%?
  **c)** What map evidence is there that part of the wetland area has been artificially drained? Describe where on the map this has happened.

**2 a)** Using extract C, list the three environments that occur in the National Park.
  **b)** In what part of the Park would you expect to find the sand dunes? (Map A on page 20 will help.)

# Coto de Doñana sanctuary is drying up

The Coto de Doñana – Spain's world famous **wetland** and one of Europe's most important wildlife sanctuaries – is in danger of drying up. This National Park contains areas of marsh, coastal woodlands, and sand dunes, and hosts as many as 150 000 wintering waterbirds. It is one of the last natural habitats of the endangered Spanish lynx and the rare imperial eagle.

For centuries the Coto de Doñana remained undisturbed. But it is now threatened by intensive rice cultivation, pollution by insecticides and fertilizers, and increased recreational activities.

▲ **C** *Extract adapted from World Wide Fund for Nature newsletter*

## Farming, tourism, or conservation?

Farmers in Andalusia use ground water to irrigate their crops. Irrigation is very wasteful. A lot of water evaporates and some soaks down through the sandy soil. Pumping water from underground is expensive, too. Farmers need more and more water to grow more crops. This could greatly lower the level of the **water table**, and cause serious environmental problems, as diagram D shows.

Tourism would bring much needed work and money into an area of high unemployment. A new tourist resort has been proposed at Matalascanas. New hotels, villas, and roads would have a visual impact on the Park. Tourists would also need more water, they use on average nearly 300 litres of water per day. At the moment this water is preserving the Doñana National Park.

▲ **D** *How the over use of ground water changes the environment*

**3** There is to be a public meeting to discuss development of the Doñana National Park. Working in groups of three, you should prepare speeches to deliver to the meeting.

One person should represent the farmers, one the owner of a hotel company, and one a conservationist who wants to preserve the area. After your debate, write up an account of the main arguments that people used.

# Catalonia – Spain's richest region

Catalonia is the richest and most industrialized part of Spain. The region covers only 6% of the country but produces 20% of its wealth. The population of Catalonia is concentrated in the coastal areas and in the city of Barcelona. The Pyrenees mountains form a dramatic border with France to the north. In the south the River Ebro meanders across the wide and rather dry landscape until it reaches its delta on the coast of the Mediterranean Sea, as you can see in map extract C.

## Using up the water resource

As in Andalusia, there is a water resource problem in Catalonia. Most rain falls in the north and west, where average rainfall is over 1000mm a year. Most people live on the coast, which is the driest part of the region with only 400mm of rainfall a year. The rivers Llobregat and Ebro carry water through Catalonia, and water is abstracted (taken out) for farming, industries, and the cities. More and more water is needed as farmers irrigate more land and new industries also demand more water. Demand for water is also increasing from new tourist developments for swimming pools, showers, baths, etc.

▼ **A** *The Pyrenees in Spain*

▲ **B** *Catalonia*

**1** Use map C.
  **a)** In which direction does the River Ebro flow
    i) in Tortosa?
    ii) where it reaches the sea?
  **b)** Sketch the delta of the Ebro. Label:
    • the river channel
    • the lagoons of water
    • the land that has been deposited by the river.

▼ **C** *The River Ebro and its delta at 1:500 000*

# Barcelona

Welcome to Barcelona! Our city is set on the beautiful coast of the Mediterranean Sea. The city sits on a gentle south-eastern facing slope, with a mild pleasant climate and the Tibidabo Mountains providing a spectacular backdrop. The fine wide streets, impressive buildings, the large public parks, and the many museums of fine art make Barcelona the second city of Spain and the cultural centre of Catalonia.

▲ F *Square in central Barcelona*

▲ D

Barcelona's population grew rapidly in the 1960s and early 1970s, as graph G shows. Most of the people who moved to the city came from rural parts of Spain. Some were forced to live in poor shanty housing, as you can see in photo E. A survey of the largest shanty in 1981 found that 31% of the migrants had come from rural parts of Catalonia and 37% from Andalusia. Of those in work, 76% had poorly paid labouring jobs on building sites. These shanties have now been cleared. Blocks of flats have been built in their place.

### Factfile: Barcelona

- The whole city has a population of over 4 million people, with 2 million living in the centre.
- Textiles, publishing, fashion, and car production are its major industries.
- Barcelona produces 75% of all the industrial products of Catalonia.
- The 1992 Olympics were held in the city.
- It has a very famous football team!

▶ G
*The growth of Barcelona's population*

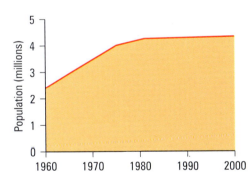

▼ E *Shanty housing in the early 1980s*

2  What makes Barcelona attractive to visitors? Use photo F to help you.

3  a) Describe the way in which Barcelona's population has grown.
   b) Why do you think it grew so rapidly in the 1970s? Use the information on this page and page 84 to help you.

4  a) Describe what you can see in photo E.
   b) What problems might people have living here?

# Industrial development in Catalonia

Most new industries in Spain have been built along the Mediterranean coast from the French border, through Barcelona, Valencia, and down to Murcia. This coastal strip produces 44% of Spanish exports.

## Barcelona – the centre of Catalonia's industry

Barcelona is the main industrial city in Catalonia. It has attracted foreign companies by offering them a site between the port and airport. Companies that locate here do not have to pay certain taxes. Tourism is also a growing industry in the city, especially since it hosted the Olympic Games in 1992. Barcelona's attractions include its medieval buildings, theatres, museums, art galleries, and opera house, as well as the nearby beach resorts.

Development has been rapid and has brought jobs and money to the city. However, this growth has caused problems for the environment. The air is polluted by car exhaust fumes and the sea by untreated sewage.

▼ **A** *The SEAT car plant*

Barcelona is trying to plan for further development, but faces a number of problems:
- control of pollution
- increasing demand for water
- lack of space because of the mountains to the north and west.

One example of a new development is the new SEAT car plant as shown in photo A. This has been built next to a rail line on the higher land behind the city.

# Spain in the wider world

Spain became a member of the European Economic Community in 1986. Before this, Spanish factories were mainly small and used out-of-date production methods. By 1990, Spain had become the eighth biggest economy in the world. This change has been brought about largely by foreign investment from companies like Ford and General Motors. Many of these companies have been attracted by Spain's low wages.

## What effect have these changes had upon wealth and poverty in Spain?

Between 1984 and 1990 the average income per person in Spain doubled. It is now US$12 460. The gap between Spain and other developed countries is closing – the average income in the UK is US$16 750 and in the USA US$22 560. Spain confidently predicts that it will catch up with the UK by the year 2000.

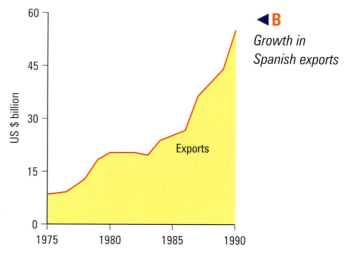

◄ **B**
*Growth in Spanish exports*

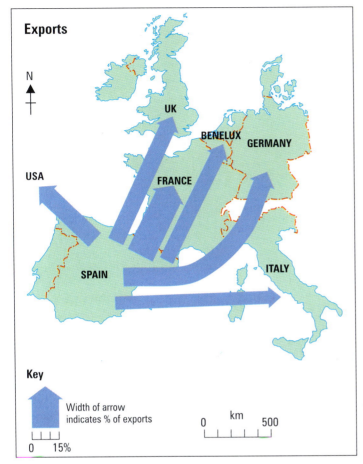

Exports

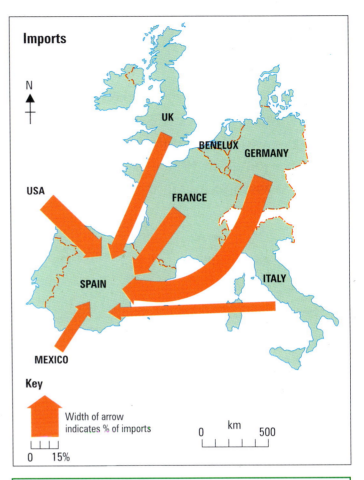

Imports

▲ C *Who does Spain trade with?*

**1** Using map C, how much of Spain's exports go to:
**a)** USA? **b)** UK? **c)** France?

**2** Describe the pattern of Spain's economic growth shown in graph B.

**3** Why is future industrial growth in Barcelona difficult? What problems will have to be overcome? Write a report for the city planners outlining the physical and environmental problems.

# Review

Spain is a country with a wide variety of landscapes. Its regions also show huge differences in the type of work they offer and their relative wealth.

Spain has undergone remarkable changes in recent times. Fewer people are employed in farming, but more land is irrigated which increases the demand for water. Service industries create 70% of Spain's wealth. Tourism is the most important of these service industries.

Tourism creates many jobs, and earns money for the country. Its rapid development has had an impact on the environment, especially by increasing the demand for water.

**4** Imagine that you have recently moved from the UK to live in Spain. Use what you have learnt in this unit to write a letter to a friend describing what Spain is like and how it is changing.

# 9 The European Union

Fifteen countries make up the European Union (EU).
Map A shows the countries that:
- were EU members in 1994
- joined in 1995
- wish to join in the future.

EUROPE

▶ A
European Union
membership

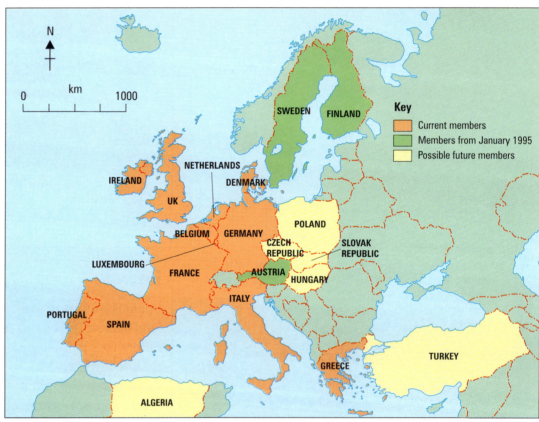

## What does the EU do?

European Union countries work together.
- They agree how much each type of farm should produce in each EU country. This makes sure that people have enough milk, wheat and vegetables. It also makes sure that farmers are paid fair prices.
- They make travel and trade easy between EU countries. This helps businesses to sell their goods.
- They help areas of high unemployment in the EU. Money is given to help development in these areas.

1 Use map A to list:
a) EU member countries
b) countries who may join.

## Helping poorer areas

Some EU countries are richer than others. As table C shows, Germany is much richer than Portugal. Some areas such as Spain, have both rich and poor areas. The EU gives money to poorer areas. These areas are either:
* industrial areas where jobs have been lost when old industries closed down
* rural areas where there are few jobs and facilities.

Merseyside in the UK receives help from the EU. It will be given £1600 million over the next five years. People can be trained in new skills and new technology to help them to find work. Transport to the area will be improved. These developments should attract new companies to the area and create more jobs.

| Current members | GNP (US $) per person | People per doctor |
|---|---|---|
| Germany | 23650 | 370 |
| Greece | 6230 | 580 |
| Ireland | 10780 | 630 |
| Italy | 18580 | 210 |
| Portugal | 5620 | 490 |
| UK | 16750 | 300 |
| **Countries which have applied to join** | | |
| Turkey | 1820 | 1260 |
| Poland | 1830 | 490 |
| Hungary | 2690 | 340 |

▲ **C** Variations in wealth between some EU countries

▼ **B** Regions of the EU that receive help

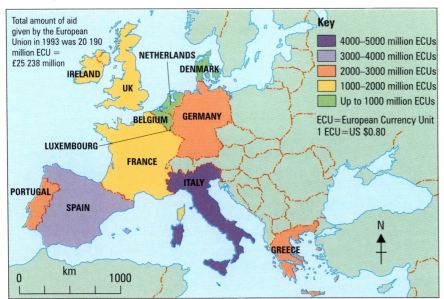

**Key**

- 4000–5000 million ECUs
- 3000–4000 million ECUs
- 2000–3000 million ECUs
- 1000–2000 million ECUs
- Up to 1000 million ECUs

ECU=European Currency Unit
1 ECU=US $0.80

Total amount of aid given by the European Union in 1993 was 20 190 million ECU = £25 238 million

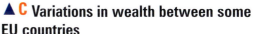

# Merseyside grasps EU lifeline

Merseyside has a terrible unemployment problem. It has been caused by the loss of unskilled jobs on the docks, and the closing down of big manufacturing companies. In Bootle, almost half the adult male population is jobless.

▲ **D** From *The Times*, 2 November 1994

**2** In which ways does the EU help poorer areas?

**3 a)** Using table B, draw a bar chart to show the wealth of Germany, Portugal, Greece, and Poland.

**b)** Copy the sentences opposite, using your chart to help choose the right words.

Germany has much *more/less* wealth than Portugal and Greece. Poland is much *richer/poorer* than many current EU members.

**4** The EU wishes to help poorer *regions* but may not want poorer *countries* like Turkey to join. Discuss possible reasons for this.

# Glossary

**Accessible**   A place that is easy to reach, usually close to good roads.

**Agroforestry**   Combining farming and forestry in a way that does not destroy the rainforest. Fruits, nuts, and firewood are harvested from the forest while crops are grown on thin strips of cleared land.

**Birth rate**   The number of babies born each year for every 1000 people.

**Canopy**   The canopy of the rainforest is the dense layer of leaves at the top of the trees. It is so thick that it cuts out most sunlight and protects the forest floor from heavy rainfall.

**Climate**   The average weather conditions of a place or region. Daily weather records are added together and the average found to give a general pattern of climate over a year.

**Colonize**   Plants do this when they take over a new patch of land.

**Conurbation**   A very large urban area created when two or more towns grow into each other.

**Coral reefs**   Corals are tiny marine animals. They often have a hard outer skeleton of limestone. They live together in large colonies which are mounded up into a reef. Coral reefs develop in warm shallow seas.

**Cyclones**   Violent storms which start over the sea in tropical regions. High winds, heavy rain, and large waves cause flooding and destruction in coastal areas.

**Deposition**   The dropping of sediment. Rivers deposit sediment on the inside bend of meanders, on their flood plains, and on the delta. The sea deposits sediment on the shore as a beach.

**Deforestation**   The cutting down of trees and clearing of forest areas. The timber may be sold or used for firewood, or the land may be needed for something else, e.g. farming or mining.

**Developed countries**   Countries with wealthy economies and a high percentage of people living in urban areas.

**Developing countries**   Countries with poorer economies where many people live in rural areas.

**Economy**   The economy of a country is its trade, industry, and money.

**Ecosystem**   A community of plants and animals, and the environment in which they live. Each part of the ecosystem depends on the other parts.

**Environment**   The surroundings in which people, animals, and plants live. It may be a natural environment such as rainforest or savanna, or an urban environment such as a city.

**Equator**   An imaginary line round the middle of the Earth which represents the $00^{\circ}$ line of latitude. It is 40076km long.

**Erosion**   The wearing away of the Earth's surface by the action of rivers, ice, sea, or the wind.

**Estuary**   The mouth of a river where fresh water meets the salt water of the sea.

**Exports**   Goods and services which are produced in one country and sold overseas to other countries.

**Fertilizers**   Manure or chemicals put on the land to enrich the soil and help plants to grow. They can increase the amount of plants and food grown.

**Firewood**   Wood collected to be used for cooking and heating

**Gross National Product (GNP)**   Is a measure of the wealth of a country. It is usually divided by the population of the country, to give a rough idea of the average wage per person.

**Habitat**   The natural environment of a plant or animal.

**Hectare**   An area of land equal to 100m x 100m.

**Hydro-electric power (HEP)**   Electricity produced by the force of fast-moving water. The power of the moving water is used to drive turbines which generate electricity.

**Igneous rock**   A crystalline rock that is resistant to erosion, such as granite.

**Imports**   Goods that are brought from another country.

**Informal work**   Work which does not have a regular wage, and where the worker does not pay taxes. Examples include selling goods on the street without a licence, or scavenging rubbish and recycling it.

**Inner city**   Housing near the centre of a city. Some inner city areas have been neglected and housing needs repair, others are being redeveloped with new housing and shops.

**Irrigate**   To transport water to an area where there is a shortage, usually to grow crops.

**Irrigation**   Transporting water to an area where there is a shortage, usually for growing crops.

**Landslide**   The sudden movement of earth and rock down a hill or mountain side. Landslides can be started by a number of things: heavy rain, deforestation, building on the slope, or erosion at the bottom of the slope.

**Life expectancy**   The number of years the average person can expect to live. This varies from one place to another according to diet, medical facilities, quality of housing, and type of work.

**Logging**   Cutting down trees for wood or timber to sell.

**Mangrove trees**   Trees which grow on tropical coastlines, where rivers enter the sea. They are the only trees that can grow in brackish water (a mixture of salt and river water). They have long roots above ground which help trap sediment.

**Manufacturing**   Making goods such as stereos, computers, televisions, cars, or parts of goods (components), e.g. computer chips or car windscreens.

**Migrants**   People who move away from their homes, usually in search of work.

**Migration**   Movement of people from one place to another, as in **Migrants** above.

**Mudslides**   Heavy rain or melting snow turns soil and rocks into flowing liquid mud.

**Nutrients**   Substances which help plants to grow, usually found naturally in the soil where the land is fertile but they are often added by farmers to make plants grow better.

**Organic farming**   No artificial fertilizers or pesticides are used.

**Plantations**   A large area of land used to grow one type of crop such as tea, sugar, coffee, cotton, or trees for timber.

**Pollution**   Contamination of water, land, or air by waste. Rubbish, sewage, industrial waste, and exhaust fumes are all examples.

**Population density**   The number of people per area of land (usually per km². ).

**Population distribution**   The pattern of where people live.

**Raw materials**   The basic natural materials needed to produce things, e.g. timber, oil, or iron ore.

**Renewable energy**   Types of energy that are produced from sources that will always be available, e.g. wave power, wind power, and tidal power.

**Rural area**   Country area where most people live in villages and small towns.

**Sanitation**   A sewage system and clean water supply.

**Savanna**   A grassy plain with few or no trees found in tropical and subtropical regions.

**Sediment**   Pieces of rock which are carried and then dropped by water, wind, or ice.

**Sedimentary rock**   Any rock formed by deposited sediment, e.g. sandstone or clay.

**Settlement**   A group of houses and other buildings. It may be just a few homes or a large city.

**Service**   Helping or serving someone, e.g. serving someone in a shop or restaurant. Service companies sell their services rather than make products, e.g. transport, banking, shops.

**Shanty town**   Another name for a squatter settlement.

**Smog**   A fog caused by damp air mixing with air pollution such as car fumes.

**Squatter settlement**   A settlement which has been built by the people who live there on land that does not belong to them.

**Storm surge**   Waves that flood coastal areas caused by a rise in the level of the sea due to strong winds.

**Tide**   The regular change in the level of the sea on the shore. The time when the level is highest is known as high tide, the lowest is low tide.

**Tropical rainforests**   Forests that grow near the Equator, where there is high rainfall and temperatures above 25°C. At least half the world's species of wildlife live in the rainforests. The largest rainforests are found in the Amazon Basin in South America and in Zaire, Africa.

**Unemployment**   People who are unable to find work.

**Urban area**   A built-up area, town, or city.

**Urban heat island**   Towns and cities are slightly warmer than the surrounding countryside because of heat radiating off roads and buildings. Heat also escapes from the buildings.

**Water table**   The level of water in the ground. The height of the water table goes up and down depending on how much rain has fallen and how much water has been taken out (abstracted).

**Weather**   The conditions of the atmosphere, such as the temperature, amount of rain, or sunshine.

**Weathering**   The breaking down of rocks caused by the effects of the weather and atmosphere.

**Wetland**   A marshy or boggy piece of land that may be flooded with water in the rainy season. Wetlands in the UK contain rare species of wildlife, but many have been ploughed up and drained to make better farmland.

# Index